THE *Punch* BOOK OF GOLF

THE *Punch* BOOK OF GOLF

Edited by **WILLIAM DAVIS**

HUTCHINSON OF LONDON

A PUNCH book, published by
HUTCHINSON & CO. (*Publishers*) LTD.
3 Fitzroy Square, London, W.1.
London Melbourne Sydney Auckland
Wellington Johannesburg Cape Town
and agencies throughout the world

First Published June 1973
Second impression November 1973
Third impression April 1974
Fourth impression April 1976
Fifth impression June 1978

Printed in Great Britain by
The Leagrave Press Ltd.
Luton and London

ISBN 0 09 116900 3

CONTENTS

Introduction

MARK TWAIN once said that golf is the silliest way of going for a walk that was ever invented, or words to that effect. He clearly didn't own a dog. But I can see what he meant: to the non-initiated anyone who regularly gets up at dawn to knock a little ball around a golf course must seem pretty daft. Golf enthusiasts could give a dozen reasons—the clean morning air, the exercise, the friendship, the challenge, the drinking, the pleasures of getting away (however briefly) from one's family. But I can't help feeling that for hard-headed Mark the best argument in favour of the game would have been that it's good for business.

Golf and money have always had a close association. Historians maintain that we owe the game to Scottish traders, who saw *chole* or some similar game played on the Continent and decided to adapt it. Later they took the game to Holland—chiefly, it is thought, because it proved an effective way to catch Dutch businessmen off guard and win profitable orders. The Americans and, more recently the Japanese made much the same discovery. A morning on the golf course is frequently more lucrative than a week in the office—and a lot more pleasant. In the office, businessmen are harassed, suspicious, and over-cautious. If they run vast corporations they are also likely to be well protected by officious secretaries and personal assistants. On the golf course they are relaxed, approachable, and receptive. But there *are* two basic rules which should never be broken. Be subtle. And don't, for God's sake, try to do business with anyone who is having a bad game. Many a promising relationship has been destroyed by crassness. People have sidled up to golf partners and tried to borrow large sums of money. Or they have eagerly pushed forward major propositions at the most unsuitable moments. Or they have made it obvious that they are deliberately losing a game for the sake of a business deal.

All such ploys invariably turn out to be self-defeating. The Golf Club is, essentially, a launching pad. It brings people together, and allows one to plant ideas. Many a merger, and many a profitable stock market deal, has started with a casual remark on the Fairway. Many ambitious executives have landed highly-paid jobs, over the heads of better-qualified rivals, by subtly developing a golf partnership. You can ring a partner up, a week later, and he will remember you. He may even invite you to his home—where, of course, you will do your best to impress him with your business talents. Or he may ring you, with a request that you should meet to discuss that casual remark. Given time—and a little skill—golf can be highly lucrative, even if you never win a bet, tournament, or championship. Some of the worst golfers have made a fortune out of the game.

Whether you play golf for business or pleasure, this book is for you. Punch has been publishing articles and cartoons about golf for more than a century, and we felt it was time to put the best of them between hard covers. There are also a good many original, tongue-in-cheek contributions. There is (we hope) useful advice on gamesmanship, but the main objective has been to provide a bit of fun. Give a copy to your bank manager or chairman; it could turn out to be an excellent investment.

WILLIAM DAVIS

"If it comes to that I haven't seen much of you at the golf-club recently."

IT ISN'T A GAME, IT'S AN ART

Why else do you need so many clubs? Asks PETER BLACK

IT must be forty years since I picked up an old cleek belonging to my father and swung at a golf ball with it; and, Lord, the changes I have seen. Why, there must be quite a few readers who were stumped just by the word cleek. It was a fairly straight-bladed iron with a fairly shallow face, and you used it when you wanted to hit a low, boring shot into the wind. Now the cleek, so far as it exists at all, is called the number one iron. The numbering of clubs came in with the steel shaft and the possibility of manufacturing matched sets, and I often meet young sparks who wonder what the old fool is rambling on about with his talk of brassies, spoons, mashies and niblicks. The only club to have kept its name is the putter.

Golf was never as snobbish as outsiders thought. I remember a scene at St. George's Hill before the war when a dentist was elected captain against the wishes of a determined bloc who saw in this event the shadow of the tumbrils. It was always hard to get into the kind of golf club James Bond belonged to, and still is. Swinley Forest, near Ascot, limits its membership to two hundred and has, I believe, a ten-year waiting list. But there were always middle and lower class clubs, where the members played in cycle clips with their trousers tucked into their socks, and called each other Mister.

On the whole, though, golf has moved with the times. The snobbery has altered its stance. The questions now are Who do you know? and Can you afford it? not, What do you do? and What was your school? Alongside this, as you would expect, there's been a sharp decline in observance of golf etiquette. The bastards won't let you through.

It is a much harder game than it used to be. Until 1950 the par of a course was based on the score a reasonably average golfer would achieve if he made no mistakes. Now the par is based on the absurd prognosis that on top of making no mistakes he can hit a ball two hundred and fifty yards. The result of this has been the disappearance of all those better than scratch handicaps, the Plus Two, Three, even Four men that used to figure on the trophy boards.

It's cleaner, too, thanks to the influence of televised golf. When I was a boy only a handful of golfers ever saw Bobby Jones, Henry Cotton, Gene Sarazen, Walter Hagen, and half a hundred more that I could name without needing a reference book. Today everyone knows Jack, Gary, Arnie and Jacko; and their presence on the box has transformed the look and odour of golf. Golfers look prettier and smell nicer. The fragrance of old shoes and sweaters that used to give men's locker-rooms their peculiar atmosphere has given way to the whiff of Brut and Old Spice and talcum powder.

The central truth of golf, though, remains the same. It isn't really a game; it's an art.

If it were a game, played at an unreflective speed, such as hockey, you would use one club only. Most golfers carry fourteen for the same reason that a painter's easel can accommodate fourteen or more brushes; they are not too many for the delicate, varied and agonisedly solitary and introspective making of strokes.

It is the introspection that makes the art. The actual swing of a golf club at a ball is no more complicated physically than the act of swinging an axe at a selected spot

on a tree. There's nothing to it. Max Faulkner told me once that by the time a good golfer had passed his twentieth birthday he should have trained his muscles to deliver the perfect swing every time. (We all show this perfect command of muscle memory every time we drop a finger unerringly on the light switch in the middle of the night.) In theory, said Max, all you needed to do was to switch your mind off, first telling your muscles to get on with it. It is because you cannot switch off your mind, because under pressure it transmits the possibility of failure to the muscles, that competitive golf, even on the level of the monthly medal, tests will and determination more than beef and co-ordination. The art is in willing the muscles to stop fooling.

Bobby Jones's swing was the perfection of drowsy elegance, as Bernard Darwin called it. But when he won the British Open in 1930 he fought round the seventy-two holes without ever, as Darwin wrote, playing really well. Most of the time he was retrieving errors. He said in his book, *Bobby Jones On Golf*, that of all the rounds of golf he'd played only five had been easy—five times when, as he put it, "I had to make no special effort to do anything."

Now, the unique appeal of golf, the thing that keeps you at it, is that it is impossible to play eighteen holes without playing one shot as well as Bobby Jones could have done it, even though it may only be the holing of an eight-foot putt and of no more significance than leaving a good set of footprints in a sand trap. Everyone can do it right sometimes. It seems intolerable not to do it always. No; not just intolerable: shameful; humiliating; undeserved.

I used to mind playing badly so much that a miasma of gloom appeared to play about my head, rather like the unholy nimbus with which early painters surrounded the head of the foul fiend. I no longer burn, but I have compassion for those who do. I was playing one day last summer with an Australian, normally a strong, steady golfer, whose game had become so unhinged that he was incapable of doing more than disturb the ball a few yards. After one such blow that must almost have dislocated his shoulderblades he took off his Gary Player-type cap, lifted his eyes skywards and said: "You work hard all the week. You look forward to your golf. All you want is to enjoy your one afternoon out. And what happens? You get *punished!*" I thought he expressed himself delicately and truthfully.

You have noticed that without actually saying so, I have suggested to you that I am very good at golf. Well, it's quite true. I am extremely good; and it's a constant puzzle to me why I don't play better. With this admission we approach the inner truth of golf. *Golfers mind playing badly because it seems an unjust reflection of their normal game.*

Henry Longhurst rouses much bitterness in his golf commentaries on TV by constantly drawing attention to what his audience does not in its bones accept—that there is a difference between the way they can play and the way Gary, Jack and Arnie can. "This is just the kind of shot the club golfer dreads," Henry will say as Palmer shapes up to a pitch over a bunker. "He knows he'll pop it into the sand."

"*It's only a* game, *Marion.*"

Not true. The club golfer looks forward keenly to such a shot. He sees it clearly with his inner eye. Perfectly struck, the ball thumps down by the flag and squirms to a stop. The only thing is, just that once he didn't hit it right. But to say that he can't is ridiculous.

The multi-million pound golf industry refutes the learned Longhurst. The accessory and clothing industry could not have flourished (it is of course based on one of the oldest myths, that one can acquire strength by eating the strong) if golfers did not know in their hearts that they were good players having an off day. There would be no point in buying a set of Lee Trevino woods if they couldn't use them; they might just as well stick to their old Jack Nicklaus's. A more striking example is the success of the books. Every instructional book ever written about golf assumes that the reader can do what it says. "For the fade shot," wrote Bill Cox in his Penguin, *Improve Your Golf*, "the ball should be played from just inside the left heel with the stance very slightly open." Tommy Armour's *How To Play Your Best Golf All The Time* was based on the principle of placing each shot to set oneself up well for the next. The ingenious Tommy knew he could rely for sales on every golfer's belief that he can hit the ball where he's aiming.

And there's a kind of logic—perhaps the truth within the inner truth—that says Armour is right. Sometimes you can split every fairway with a stroke that looks, feels and sounds triumphantly right. Next week it will have gone. But it is still there, somewhere; and it's no more absurd to believe that the good swing was the normal one, and the other is some demoniac intervention, than to put it the other way round.

"How about it . . . I won't mention anything if you don't?"

OUT OF THE ROUGH

R. G. G. PRICE turns an inexpert but fascinated eye on Golf's past

GOLF historians take tremendous pride in the ancienty of their sport. One of them claims, with a dramatic lack of hedging, that it was prehistoric in origin. If there is a *Cambridge History of Golf*, with bibliographies, I haven't seen it, I'm glad to say, but, in the books that I *have* found, patriotic Scots seem rather worried by the possible debt of the game to a Dutch diversion called *kolf*. There were, even its supporters admit, certain differences. For instance it was played in a long shed, eighty feet by twenty on a hard floor. There were posts and holes and, to me, it sounds more like a mixture of croquet, hockey, ninepins and bowls. (The Dutch, by the way, "played a less frantic kind of *kolf* than the Belgians".)

Most writers prefer to believe that it descended from the stone age via the Celts, who often give the impression that they were prehistoric later than other nations. It is true that the early Celtic game does not sound much fun; but then there is no evidence that it was supposed to be an amusement. What does seem firm ground is that Golf emerges from its mists in the fifteenth century, when Kings of Scotland, though indulging feverishly themselves, tried to discourage their subjects because it distracted them from archery and hence from practising for defence. No invading army would be deterred by being driven into. James II of Scotland (or minus IV of England) got a subservient parliament to command that "the Fute-ball and Golf be utterly cryit doune and nocht to be usit." Nobody took much notice and the bow-makers moved into the clubmaking trade.

For centuries Golf remained a private possession of the Scots. Mary, Queen of ditto, played it in the gardens of Seaton House, Montrose played it, the Young Pretender and his brother, the future Cardinal of York, played it in the Borghese Gardens.

I don't mean that it was unheard of in England; but it was only a report from the wild north. However, I should honestly mention that Garrick once invited his friends to a golf-party. As they passed through Kensington on their way, the Coldstream Regiment were changing guard and, seeing their clubs, gave three cheers in honour of a diversion peculiar to Scotland. What gives this idiotic anecdote an extra something is that Andrew Lang, from whom I have pinched it, with much else, dates the party to 1798, while Garrick died in 1779. Well, Lang always did like a ghost story.

Scottish pastimes tend towards the arduous and the grim. This may seem a misleading description of a game that is associated nowadays with luxurious clublife, mechanised transport along the course and mergers settled on the green; but in its heartland it was played the hard way. Through the seamists, with eyes sharpened by stalking the wiry stag, dour, hairy men peered forward and hit their balls into the teeth of gales as they edged the match towards a sourly greeted victory.

Early golf was only a few club-lengths inland from French cricket. The dictionary definition of a "link" is "Comparatively level or gently undulating sandy ground covered with turf or coarse grass." In Sussex, by the way, the word meant a "green or wooded bank between two pieces of cultivated ground." Just as well that Golf didn't originate down south.

The Royal & Ancient club of St. Andrews is set amid a cheerless mixture of dunes, spray and coarse, sea-marginal grasses. Golf was played there certainly before 1557. A high proportion of the earliest members came from the University. (This connection between groves and greens has persisted.) In James II's time there was a "forecadie" who ran in front to mark the ball down but gradually the decay of the whins made him superfluous. Vegetation provided much of the irritant in early golf. In 1743, a long poem, *The Goff*, by Thomas Matheson sings,

> The creeping ball its want of force complains,
> A grassy tuft the loitering orb detains.

As late as the end of the next century, there were still complaints about "deplorable commons where the hazards are whins and the green is a foot deep in vegetation." All the same, already, by the mid-eighteenth century, about 100 to 105 was an average winning score at St. Andrews so, if the course was far from fast, it wasn't impenetrable.

Golf spread, though slowly. An informal club existed at Pau in the 1850s. The Blackheath Club, originally called "the Knuckle Club", was, in some moods, capable of claiming to have been founded by England's first Stuart King; but one of my more downright sources says firmly that Golf was brought south in 1863 by General Moncrieffe and where he brought it to was *Westward Ho*, an estate named after Kingsley's stirring tale of how stout Protestants saved us from evil Catholics. It seems probable, though I can't exactly prove it, that this was the only course named after fiction. (Surely not St. Andrews?) The first imported pro was John Allan. Thrawn golf pros, and thrawn gardeners, brought with them the puritanism of their native heather: they firmly stopped their employers from degrading duty into mere pleasure.

Some of the details I have gleaned seem odd to me, though they may strike addicts as quite ordinary. A medieval bishop who was playing golf saw two men pursuing him with swords, though nobody else saw them. He cast away his clubs, went home to bed instantly and died, "without giving any token of repentance for that wicked course he had embraced." In the Amateur Championship of 1888 a player hit his ball into a spectator's pocket. A man who was driven into ordered his caddy to tee the offender's ball and drove it into the sea. A stranger making up a four tried to putt through a large, black dog. On being assured that it was real, he confessed that the fine air had led him to take a glass of port after his cheese for two or three days, which had never agreed with him.

After the early days, clubs grew lighter and their heads smaller. "Gutties" were replacing feather-cored, leather-cased balls by 1848. In the 1870s, clubs in use at Westward Ho! were: Driver or play-club, long spoon, mid-spoon, short spoon, the "grass" or "grassed" club, which came between driver and long spoon, wooden putter, driving putter (for driving the ball against the wind when there were no bunkers), irons, which the Scots brought to England, viz cleek, driving iron, lifting iron and niblick, which was not much use for lofting, as its head was smaller than the ball. There was no mashie or brassie. The later brassie was a wooden club with brass on the sole for use on rutted roads. Rutted *roads?* Yes. The idea of a course right away from life's traffic grew slowly. Balls cost 1/- and machine-hammered balls superseded idented ones. By the way, the statement that the baffy had passed out of common use by the 1870s is not quite accurate. When I was a child in West Dulwich, my aunt kept a baffy in the hall for fear of cat burglars, then quite a feature of urban living.

In the earliest code of the R & A, the tee had to be on the ground and within a club's length of the hole. The name comes from the letter 't' and meant originally a mark made on the ice for curling. The use of sand to give you an advantage was as bad as a revoke. Fairway comes from "Fareway", a navigable channel. Before I leave the last century, two topics deserve a mention, Competitions and Women. The Open began at Prestwick in 1860. If the same winner won the belt three years running, he kept it and the competition lapsed. The American Open started in 1894. In 1902, the British champion used the new rubber-cored ball. So much for fact: now for Women.

Although in the 1770s Musselburgh offered a creel and a shawl to the best golfer among the fishwives, ladies were not generally welcomed on courses. They used to be hooted off with cries of "Fore!" Lord Wellwood, writing at the end of the last century, advised that, for the newly established Ladies' Links, seventy or eighty yards should be the average limit of a drive, as that could be carried without raising the club above the shoulder. "The posture and gesture requisite for a full swing are not particularly graceful when the player is clad in female dress." Ladies should play only when male golfers were feeding or resting. However, at least they were less nuisance as players than as spectators, when not merely did they chatter but the shadow of their dresses was apt to flicker on the putting-green. *They should never be allowed to score.*

The chapter on "The Humours of Golf" in the *Badminton Library* volume is by Balfour. How on earth did he ever become the tame wit of the Souls? Perhaps it was ghosted by the Civil Service.

This century, grass has become more disciplined, clubhouses more hotel-like, their bars more sparkling and ambitiously stocked, standards of play ever following professional standards upwards and facilities discovered to serve not merely the needs

"Get on with your work, Gregston!"

of exercise but socioeconomic ends, a term unknown to the be-knighted Lord Wellwood. Almost as important today is the local pecking-order aspect: a man's status can be affected by which club in an area has accepted him and status, in a credit-conscious world, can affect his financial position.

The money to be made out of the game has increased enormously. There are more and more saleable gadgets, more and more plushy job covering the game for the media, more and more for builders, decorators, furnishers and wine merchants, more and more books on how to improve your game, and more and more fees to be made from strains, sprains, slipped discs and, in the game's northern home, frostbite.

This century has seen many advances in golf technology, not all of which caught on, e.g. the pneumatic ball, which had a tendency to explode. It has also seen the rise of the golf star, insisting on being treated as a top line entertainer, not as a servant, and making a fortune. Hagen, with his genial gamesmanship, his showbiz flourishes, his unapologetic zest for money, his union of ball-control and tactical skill and his entry into the magic circle of millionaires, was a different breed from the whiskery ex-caddies who were as frank as ghillies during play and as proletarian and invisible as grooms after it.

This development, as in the similar development in Boxing, raised standards of average performance and, despite some vulgarisation, the balance of advantage was with the new relationships between expertise and publicity. If the various newspaper proprietors, equipment manufacturers, television technicians, commentators made money as well as the champions, surely it was an innocent method of making it. Golf is a rather clean game and the more cameras there are trained on the players, the less chance there is of cooking a tournament. Well, how would *you* set about doping Jack Nicklaus or substituting a "ringer" for Gary Player or getting at Arnold Palmer's clubs and making the heads waggle?

"Simmer down, Hayward—we all have days when we can't do a thing right."

"Fore!"

Nippon Golf

BILL TIDY follows the new Japanese religion.

"No . . . remove cap when addressing ball."

"No, No! Not big championship. Members waiting for a game."

"*Please do not bother to remove footmarks. Mr. Nakamura is world famous sand garden artist.*"

"*Please ignore . . . has been lurking in thick rough on 15th fairway for twenty-eight years.*"

"Do we have the Tee Ceremony at every hole?"

"Excuse please. Do you mind if we play through?"

"What do you mean 'in short rough'? Those are trees."

"No. 11 please."

We Have Ways of Spoiling Your Swing

BEN WRIGHT on the golfer's psyche.

IF one is prepared to believe the oft-advanced theory that golf is at least 75 per cent a mental game and not, as non-golfers would have it a disease of the mind, then the art of "psyching" the opposition has a very real place in the scheme of things.

The important point at issue is to decide where skilful and amusing gamesmanship ends and unfair conduct, or cheating begins. If the gamesmanship is crude and unsubtle, as it was when Tommy "Thunder" Bolt, the great American professional strolled on to the first tee in the Ryder Cup match at Lindrick in 1957 and hissed: "Your beat, sucker", to his British opponent, Scotsman Eric Brown, it deserves to backfire—and on this occasion thankfully did so with a vengeance. Far from being intimidated or put off Brown, just the wrong man to attempt to get at in this way, carried the verbal fight to the opposition to such a good effect he ran out an easy winner of this, the top single by 4 and 3, and set Britain on the way to a famous victory—her only postwar success in this biennial fixture which has since established an unenviable reputation for such verbal fisticuffs.

Of course some golfers fall easy prey to their opponents' "psyching" technique. In Frank Beard's brilliant, subsequently published diary called "Pro", a day-by-day description of life on the American tour in 1969, when he finished leading money winner, Beard tells an engaging tale of how Harold "The Horse" Henning regularly psychs his more talented countryman from South Africa, Gary Player.

"When I'm playing Gary head to head in a tournament", Henning told Beard, "I'll walk up to him on the tee and say: 'Gary, you don't look well. Do you feel all right? Have you lost some weight? Have you been ill?'

"Immediately Gary starts worrying. 'Do you really think so?' he says. 'Do I look ill?'

"From then on, he's mine. Just make a reference to his health, and that will take care of him every time".

As a renowned former hypochondriac myself I have to admit that I have been similarly psyched many times, and many more in more subtly insidious ways, nor am I snow white and innocent of much the same tactics in reverse. One of the most difficult tasks for a weekend golfer to accomplish is to finish off his man in matchplay. The natural, if subconscious inclination is to ease up a little once you get a few holes in front. Before you know where you are your victim has staged a notable comeback, and you're walking down the last fairway all square, and considerably shaken. And that sinking feeling tells you he's got the initiative now. It is surprising, or is it, how a sudden twinge of acute backache when your position is apparently hopeless will soften up the shortly-to-be-triumphant opposition with dramatically effective swiftness . . .

I recently employed a tactic passed on to me by cartoonist David Langdon, with conspicuously successful results. The ploy is executed on the putting green when your opponent is faced by a sizeable putt, and your own ball is much nearer to the hole, but at a complete tangent. As the opposition prepares to putt you ask politely if you should mark and remove the nearer ball, although it is plainly not anywhere near interfering in any way either physically, or on the line of sight. Your opponent, nonplussed by the apparent stupidity of your suggestion, is caught perfectly in two minds. He tells you shortly not to bother, and then you can read his innermost thoughts almost as if they were spoken. "Why the hell did he ask me that damn fool question?" Concentration should be broken completely. If it isn't, it very soon will be if the ploy is repeated at regular intervals.

Many world class professionals are in the same league in the field of gamesmanship. One such veteran I know well, and who shall be nameless, always asks on the first tee to see the driver of any young and inexperienced player with whom he is drawn to play. He addresses an imaginary ball with the club in question, makes a face expressing a combination of distaste and disbelief, and without a word hands back the offending weapon. The damage is most effectively achieved without a word being spoken.

Lee Trevino is acknowledged as the world's leading gamesman, or as the Americans call it "hustler" of his age, which is hardly surprising in view of his background. An illegitimate child brought up by his grandfather, a gravedigger in Dallas, Texas, the Mexican-American Trevino graduated to "hustling" naturally as a means of dragging himself a notch or two up the social scale from the extreme poverty bracket so despised in that part of the world. Quickly he established a nationwide reputation as a golfing genius, even when using a quart-sized "Dr. Pepper" bottle, the doctor in question being the brand name of a soft drink with which Trevino struck up only a nodding acquaintance—he preferred margaritas. Trevino, who had bound the bottle with adhesive tape, would challenge all comers to matches for money at the Tennison Park municipal course in which he drove with this bizarre "club"—and most often won.

When he graduated to a "legitimate" and meteoric career in major tournament and championship golf Trevino's constant chatter with both crowds and partners endeared himself at least to the former. It was interpreted as a safety valve, a means of dissipating extreme nervousness. Trevino's humour and ready wit made him the leading character in world class golf. But after the recent Piccadilly World Matchplay Championship at Wentworth I was not alone in questioning Trevino's motives.

Is the chatter quite so innocent and unrehearsed, as delightfully spontaneous as it appears?

I was first shocked by Trevino's typically frank and honest admission in a bar in Miami in March, 1970 that he had "got at" Sukree Onsham, the diminutive Thai of minimal international experience who came so near to beating the brilliant Mexican-American for individual World Cup honours the previous November in Singapore.

With three holes to play in the final round Trevino, whose strength is miraculous, admitted to having been practically out on his feet. He had travelled to the immense heat of the east from the cool west coast of America after his amazing collapse over the last three holes of the Alcan championship in Portland, Oregon.

"I felt so whacked out that to talk Sukree out of it seemed to be about my only chance", Trevino told me then.

The wily Lee thereupon walked over to Onsham, slapped him on the back, and said: "Sukree, you fine, great golfer. You no win anything big yet, eh? Soon you win. Sukree, champion of the whole world".

The enormity of such an achievement was something the tiny Thai had obviously not cared to think about. His game suddenly came apart at the seams, and Trevino duly became World Champion, although this is only a hollow title. In all fairness to him I have to add that "Supermex", as Trevino is affectionately known, gave away all his prize money in Singapore to set up a scholarship for caddies. The man is generous to a fault.

That same week in Miami Trevino won the $40,000 first prize in the National Airlines Open, beating Bob Menne from Andover, Massachusetts at the second hole of a sudden death play-off. The almost unheard-of Menne led from the start of the tournament, only to be caught by Trevino in the third round. When the pair remained deadlocked at the end of the fourth day Trevino told me how he might possibly talk his inexperienced rival out of the play-off.

He explained: "I'll look at Menne's strong grip on the first tee and say: 'Bob, you've done really well to stand up to all this pressure this week when you've never won before, especially with a grip like that'. He should pretty soon hook one after that".

When the play-off took place Trevino came in right on cue, just as he had rehearsed the speech. And just as he expected Menne hooked his way out of $40,000 at the second hole.

On relating this story to several British professionals, I was told several times that the individuals concerned would have punched Trevino on the nose in similar circumstances.

In the recent Piccadilly semi-final clash between Trevino and his arch rival Tony Jacklin the latter told me at lunchtime that he was furious with himself because once again he had allowed his opponent's chatter to get to him. We all know the end of the story, of how not even an incredibly brilliant second round of 63 could save Jacklin from defeat at the last of 36 holes, because he had given his conqueror a prodigally extravagant four up start at half time.

At a dinner party during the Swiss Open in Crans-sur-Sierre a fortnight after this year's British Open at Muirfield, won by Trevino, Jacklin had told me how he was still not sure whether or not Trevino had talked him out of the championship in that instance. Then it was that the pair walked down the 17th fairway on the final afternoon, with Trevino muttering far from quietly after he had hooked his drive into a bunker. Trevino said then—and I heard every word—that he had "blown" the championship because a photographer had broken his concentration, and caused him to step away from his ball on the tee. Trevino played three casual shots after that hurtful drive without ever threatening to stay on the fairway or the green, but in effect it was Jacklin's concentration that was broken, and he who threw away a title he appeared to have firmly in his grasp—when Trevino miraculously chipped his ball straight into the hole for the most astonishing par five.

Jacklin also recalled that evening how, when paired with Trevino at Royal Birkdale during the 1971 British Open—which Trevino also won—Lee had talked of going home at the end of the third round. Trevino had been upset by a minority section in a huge crowd who had cheered when he missed his putts or played the occasional wayward shot. Trevino muttered darkly all the way down the 8th fairway, took three putts to drop his third shot in three holes, and Jacklin went past him with a magnificent birdie three. Tony recalled how he had been affected and upset by the situation, how he had dropped his guard, lost his concentration, and finished the round a shot behind his partner.

I leave it to you, the reader to decide whether all this is sheer coincidence or a series of deep, heinous plots dreamed up by Trevino to unhinge his British rival. But I cannot resist giving you the results of a poll conducted two years ago by the British golf magazine Golf World. In the appropriate section not one professional admitted to having descended to the use of gamesmanship on any of his rivals, but more than 70 per cent claimed that it had been used on them!

"Look sir, if this is going to leave you gentlemen short . . ."

GOLF: HOW TO AFFORD IT

Once more the high golf season is waning, and once more you're still on the outside looking in. Why? The chances are you've heard a lot of alarmist talk about the cost. Forget it, says DAVID LANGDON.

The Lessons

The teach-yourself method is cheapest. The economy-size golfer only needs a nearby course and a green-fee to get that occasional clean, sweet shot right down the middle that makes it all worth while. What if it *was* an accident? Some fools pay pounds for tuition and don't get any more clean, sweet ones than you do for nothing. They go into department store basements, hung with nets like a scene from Billy Budd, and make fifty air shots off coconut matting. Why not do it off real grass, without a pro standing over you, yawning and making you nervous?

The Lessons

"All you've got to think of is the overlapping grip fingers making Vs pointing over right shoulder left arm straight knees slightly bent ball off left heel chin pointing at ball head perfectly still club head resting natural slow back swing shoulder and hip pivot . . ."

The Clubs

Granted, you'll want one or two of these. And a mere mention will stop the pro yawning. He sells them. That's what he's a pro at, so look out you don't get landed with a matched set of true-tempered, all-weather, gripsteel-shafted. You can't afford them, and you don't need them. You'd do just as well with a few odd well-tried hickory ones inherited from an uncle, and this will cut down the outgoings considerably. Or you can keep your ears open for the owner of a matched set at 70 gns. throwing them down in the rough and announcing that he's leaving them there for ever. But a word of warning: he sometimes comes back.

The Balls

The unwritten rule that you mustn't pick up another player's ball on fairways—should you by chance find yourself in those parts—is a great character-builder. Men of honour have stooped to a spanking new four-and-ninepenny Dunlop 65, after a quick look round the empty distances. Don't. When your conscience asserts itself you'll feel an awful fool taking it into a police station. Balls pulled or sliced into thickets are different, and fair game. Join the bands of ferret-faced men who know the richest spots, and get there first, claiming to identify the find by a secret mark as one you lost last week. In case of argument, show them a shilling. If you lose twelve per round at this price you're still solvent.

The Balls

"*Make, type, serial number, any other distinguishing marks?*"

The Caddies

Forget all you've heard about these tyrants. Now that you can hire a caddy-cart for 2*s*., who's going to hire a caddy for 12*s*. 6*d*? It's hard, but they had it coming to them, with their superior airs. Walk purposefully past them, as they train a hypnotic eye on you from their seedy *kraal*. A moment's weakness, and you'll be hiring a caddy *and* a caddy-cart, the one to push the other. It is such *folies de grandeur* that push costs up.

The Clothes

Don't buy any. Golf is the one game that the correct costume and equipment won't help you to play better. Once again, the pro is the Tempter. He not only sells golf shirts, golf caps, golf gloves, golf socks, golf trousers, golf jackets and golf shoes with fringed tongues: he wears them, each item mysteriously one cut above the quality on offer, and no one knows where the pro does his own shopping, or why his stuff is always immaculate yet never quite new. Leave the puzzle unsolved, anyway, and stick to your second-best grey flannels tucked into your old brown stockings. In this rig, all other things equal, you'll play as well as the next beginner in the matching cap and tweeds . . . and should some devil tempt you to try and join a Club, the Secretary will give you one look and a personal blackball. A great saving.

The Membership

"He pays green-fees. His membership was turned down."

The Clothes

The Hole-in-One

"Now don't be ruddy ridiculous . . . Sir."

The Hole in One

This is a risk you have to take. Face up to it bravely. If you hole in one without witnesses you may get away with it. Otherwise it means a bottle of Scotch for the well-dressed strangers in the club-house, the necktie of the Hole-in-One Club, and for all I know an annual subscription to that Club's monthly magazine. Entertain no false hopes of never holing in one. It happens. And in trying to avoid it you may do it. If you can do it and not mention it, this is another mark of character well and truly built through golf.

The Membership

Hold hard to non-involvement. Actually join a Club, and all your economies in clubs, balls, caddies and clothes can vanish in the twinkling of a cheque. Putting the entrance fee at £30 and the sub at £25, and making a short mental calculation, you'll see that you're forking out in one burst enough hard cash to pay for over a hundred rounds at 10*s*. pay-as-you-go green-fee. Stick to your uncle's clubs, play with repaints, avoid the pro, spurn the caddy, wear what you wear to clean the car in, and you can be a golfer yet. Other golfers, it's true, won't speak to you. But even that could be a saving in the end.

"*Don't you* ever *relax, J.B.?*"

HOW TO PERFECT YOUR GAME

Chris Plumridge

ALL good golf books carry an instructional section and this one is no exception. To obtain maximum benefit from the instructions laid down here, firstly open the book at this page, hold the left hand side in the left hand and right hand side in the right hand, keep both eyes on the word you are trying to read and start reading from the extreme left. If you do not understand any of the instruction, our explanatory rates commence at £1.50 per hour.

FAULT	CURE
Failing to win the toss to determine the honour on the 1st tee.	Mr. Ray Illingworth, the England cricket captain, holds the world record for winning tosses in Test matches and is available for a nominal fee during the winter months only.
Bicycle clips not keeping trousers tucked in socks.	You are obviously using cheap, mass-produced Japanese clips. Buy 'Bulldog' clips, made in Birmingham—remember, British is best.
Failing to make contact with the ball.	This is known as the rabbit-syndrome and stems from a deep-seated fear of violence. Consult your psychiatrist.
Losing balls in the rough on the right of the fairway.	Aim left.
Losing balls in the rough on the left of the fairway.	Aim right.
Losing balls in the middle of the fairway.	You are playing the wrong hole or the wrong ball.
Persistent skying of tee shots.	You are trying to ensure your place in the heavenly order of things. Unless you are scratch or better you are unlikely to get in and even then you'll have to know somebody.
Your large family prevents you from getting off to play golf.	Whatever it is you've got, it ain't rhythm.
Inability to get out of bunkers.	Your technique must be wrong. First belay yourself firmly at the base and, using pitons and crampons, slowly get out. Special instruction can be had at the Dougal Halston School of Bunker Extraction, Katmandu, Nepal.

FAULT	CURE
Inability to distinguish between professional golf and amateur golf.	Professional golf is a game for idiots played by professionals and amateur golf is a game for idiots played by stockbrokers, solicitors and company chairmen.
Inability to win.	Cheat.
Unable to put back-spin on 3-iron shots.	How far do you hit a 3-iron? About 180 yards you say? Well, what do you want to stop it for?
Unable to score less than 8 on any hole.	Sink a 20-foot putt for a 7.
Missing short putts.	Never leave yourself a putt of under 4 feet, all putts over 4 feet are not considered short.
Difficulty in following the flight of the ball during televised golf tournaments.	Go to your television set, place right hand firmly on horizontal hold knob, turn slowly in anti-clockwise direction and keep eye on screen.
Flailing your shots quail-high to the left.	Since there is a dearth of quails at the moment, try flailing your shots pheasant-high to the left as they are much bigger birds and can comfortably feed a family of four.
Failing to get a decent position behind the 18th green during the last day of a golf tournament.	Like all things connected with golf, you must practise. In this case practise shoving, elbowing and queuing outside the Albert Hall, Wimbledon, Tutankhamen and Lords.
Fear of contracting the 'yips' on the putting green.	Give up reading Henry Longhurst writing about them.
Shanking or socketing.	Give up golf.
Unable to negotiate the long uphill 9th while smoking a cigarette.	Give up long hills and cigarettes.
Unable to negotiate the long uphill 9th without having a coronary.	Give up.

"Just relax J.B. I'll ring the office and get the creative boys on to the problem."

Golf Business

Mahood looks at the boom in doing business on the golf course.

"Say, does Howard Hughes play golf?"

"My goodness, business must be booming!"

"I joined the club to increase my business contacts and then discovered they have no Jewish members."

"Amalgamated's goods may be shoddy, and their delivery dates unreliable, but their Chairman knows when to concede a putt!"

"And now gentlemen, we are beginning to see the fruits of our automation programme—an eighteen hole course where the old employees car park used to be."

"I don't like the look of that!"

GLOSSARY OF GOLF

Miles Kington

HOOK a cured slice
SLICE a cured hook
AIR SHOT practice swing
GUTTA PERCHA nasty stomach ache brought on by crouching too long over putts
LONGHURST interminable discussion about which is the best golf course in the world
BUNKER small, mobile sand patch which moves swiftly to meet the ball
SHORT GAME golf match in which all your balls have been lost by the tenth
BALLS see any book on golf
DEAD when your ball is so close to the hole it's not worth putting out (when this happens to your opponent's ball, it's technically called 'missable')
GREENSOME a rather poetic word meaning 'near the green', 'just off the green', 'would have been on the green but for the wet grass'
SHUT FACE most people tend to swear and break their clubs after a run of bad shots. It is much more gentlemanly to keep a shut face
DOG LEG the tendency of one leg to lift during the swing
BIRDIE i a hole that you almost eagled
ii nasty thing that flies out of the rough at the wrong moment causing a hook or slice
ALBATROSS a huge white bird that sits in flocks on the green and disturbs your concentration
FOLLOW THROUGH a technical method used by championship golfers to hole putts. It involves throwing the club away, punching the air, hurling the cap on the ground and hugging the caddy
CADDY in professional golf, the man who pulls round the name of your sponsor
NATURAL HAZARD an excrescence which makes a normally simple shot difficult e.g. a protruding stomach or opponent's multi-coloured umbrella
ROUGH sort of club member they never used to admit in the old days
FORE! a warning cry which enables golfers to run into the path of an oncoming ball
NO. 4 WOOD best bitter
DIVOT a small bunker made of soil
ROYAL AND ANCIENT a kind of old-fashioned putter which always cures a top pro's putting problems
MIXED FOURSOME one pint of bitter, one double scotch, one gin and tonic, one lager
ROUND yours
PAR a rough and ready mathematical system which enables TV commentators to convert a golf match into something to say
BOGEY something you are scared of, the next hole, the last hole, any hole
PRO/AM the airline most used for getting competitors from the Venezuelan Open on the 24th to the Hong Kong (Rothmans) on the 25th.

JUST A SHORTER PUTT WITH THEE

Alan Coren

HAD you, a week or so ago, been taking a sundown stroll through the rolling Bucks verdure with a view, perhaps, to comparing one Chalfont with another or enriching your collection of stockbrokers' house-names, you might have seen, some four or so miles from Amersham, a strange misshapen silhouette blemishing the evening horizon. There on a busty hill it stood, rooted: a gnarled thorn, you might have said to yourself, shrugging; a Saxon barrow, time-tumbled; an extravagant horse-dropping, piled and eroded by the summer wind.

Had you time on your hands, you might have gone closer: ah, you might have cried, a statue of Charles Laughton raised by the Gerrards Cross Victor Hugo Society! That fearsome hump, those twisted legs, that shoulder dropping unnervingly to the knee, counterpointing the movement of that horrible head as it wrenches unnaturally upward poking its pitiful eye at the uncaring stars, what could it be but the great hunchback himself, frozen forever by the sculptor's art?

It could be Coren practising his golf swing, that's what; as indeed it was. The fact that the figure displayed not a tremor of movement is explained by its having been practising this swing for upwards of three hours; and it had slowly come to a complete halt, in the paralysed position. Had some charitable Samaritan not come by with liniment and Scotch, it might have been there still, already a topographical conundrum fit to rank with Stonehenge and the White Horse of Uffington, and a beacon for errant gliders.

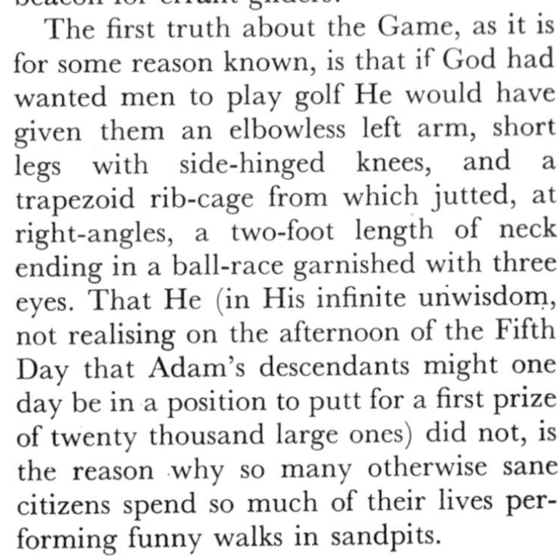

The first truth about the Game, as it is for some reason known, is that if God had wanted men to play golf He would have given them an elbowless left arm, short legs with side-hinged knees, and a trapezoid rib-cage from which jutted, at right-angles, a two-foot length of neck ending in a ball-race garnished with three eyes. That He (in His infinite unwisdom, not realising on the afternoon of the Fifth Day that Adam's descendants might one day be in a position to putt for a first prize of twenty thousand large ones) did not, is the reason why so many otherwise sane citizens spend so much of their lives performing funny walks in sandpits.

The second truth about golf is that it was entirely conceived, created and developed by manufacturers, which explains why it is that it can only be played by first distorting the human body out of all decent recognition. The *natural* way to play golf would be to throw the ball down the fairway as far as possible, walk up to it, pick it up and throw it again, and, having reached the green, throw it down the hole. However, in some far and unspecified eon, a turner with time on his hands and ineptitude on his side came up with a stick which ended in a lump, and, rather than write the thing off as a tax-loss, decided to concoct a use for it. He then drew up a list of things you could not do (all golf rules are about *not* doing things), such as throw the ball, and an industry was born, with a game as a sideline; and the profitable possibilities were endless, provided you made the game difficult enough. To take an obvious example: with the club at the prescribed height, the body is not only distorted, but incapable of natural movement unaided, except of a very limited order. It would be possible to putt, in the game's quaint parlance, but there's little money in that; so the founders decided to move the hole half a mile from the tee thereby necessitating the swing, and it is impossible to perform a swing with a hunched and broken body without falling over. Unless you have golf-shoes to tether you to the ground, at a tenner a brace, and clothes which do not fire their buttons off when the crippled hulk beneath begins to stir, like golf-jackets; and, once committed to the unnecessary club and the unnecessary swing that accompanies it if the ball is to go the unnecessary distance to the hole, you are required to purchase a pair of equally unnecessary golf-gloves, to avoid the blisters which are another thing God didn't think of back in the early days of firmanent and crawlies.

Another advantage of moving the hole away from the tee was that it rendered the single club obsolete, and forced man to accept a dozen different clubs; when this turned out to produce inadequate profits, the manufacturers went out with shovels and dug things called bunkers, which required a new kind of club altogether. It is entirely appropriate that Hitler committed suicide in one.

With all these clubs, and his body already tortured by the rules, it was immediately apparent that man was in no shape to cart the stuff around; but the benevolent manufacturers were not slow to save, being ready to offer him golf-bags, golf-trolleys, golf-karts, and caddying, which is an entirely different game, played only for money.

Having craftily arranged all this, the manufacturers sat back for a bit, to think: trade was good, the world was full of loonies prepared to subject themselves to wild expenditure, but what about progress? True, they had made the ball progressively smaller (for easier losability) with the unexpectedly profitable spin-off of the tee, which you now needed to put down in order that the tiny ball be hittable at all, but this wasn't big-league stuff, and hardly disturbed the accountants one digit.

So they invented, in 1851, the 18-hole game, with the result that the racked and abused bodies were totally incapable of getting home after a game without first dragging their cadavers into a bar and reviving them with large quantities of booze. Apart from the specific commercial benefits of this, it also fortuitously opened up an entirely new and untapped area of dormant loot: wives, suddenly finding themselves opening the door to blokes who had not only been away from home for unaccountable hours but had returned mysteriously exhausted and just as mysteriously soused, began to turn things over in their minds. And, at St. Andrews in 1872, ladies' golf was born; or, rather, ladies' clubs, shoes, clothes, karts, umbrellas, hipflasks and lessons.

Everybody, in fact, takes lessons; it being another truth about golf that, since it is an unnatural activity to start with, the player spends his life *overcoming* things—the notion that handicap is a mere numerological talking-point is ludicrous: the entire

"Promise me you won't ever try to do that."

game is shot through with, is based upon, is conceived in handicap. I have little doubt that my son, should he follow this same crazy-paved path, will be playing, a few years from now, on a forty-hole course with a regulation Royal & Ancient iron ball chained to his left leg and a book balanced on his head.

The book will undoubtedly be called HOW TO IMPROVE YOUR SWING. Ninety-eight per cent of the twelve thousand golf books produced every year are called HOW TO IMPROVE YOUR SWING. It is also the title of most of the articles written in most of the magazines and of most of the strips drawn in most of the newspapers. Occasionally, some smart fool tries to steal a march on the market by producing a book/article/strip entitled HOW TO PERFECT YOUR SWING; he is, like Byron (who played off three, despite a club foot—or, now I reflect, possibly because of it, since in a game like golf a touch of *natural* deformity probably gives you an edge over the rest of us) mad, bad, and dangerous to know: there can never be such a thing as the perfect golf swing, and to lure men on to this El Dorado with only their imperfect equipment of equal-length arms and undetachable collarbones and symmetrical eyes and articulated wrists is avaricious irresponsibility of a high and terrible order.

Hold on. It's just occurred to me—not unlike a blinding flash of pure and endless light, as a matter of fact—that I may have been doing God an injustice all this time. It was thinking of El Dorado which did it, if you're interested in the creative process. Because isn't golf a little like the image of the True Good Life Of The Spirit? Isn't an eighteen-hole course something of a Pilgrim's Progress, an analogue of Man's travail and aspiration? Perfectability is held out, not because it is achievable, but merely because it is an ever-retreating grail to be striven for, and the good man is the one who devotes himself unwaveringly to self-improvement, borne on by a distant golden promise. Right, said God, sitting back on the Seventh Day, restless in His rest after a week's hard graft at the ethereal office, we'll call it Sunday and we'll give them golf. They will all start imperfect, and I shall send them out with their imperfections, and I shall give them sand-traps and water hazards, and as soon as they are getting good or touched with pride, I shall chuck in a new obstacle, a harder hurdle. They will have days of joy, and days of despair, and each will test them in its own way, and from time to time I shall drop saints among them, Hogans and Nicklauses and the like, to point the way and offer the example, and the manufacturers shall be my interpreters, and the Royal & Ancient my Establishment from which all encyclicals issue, and the club professionals shall be my ministers, and Man and Woman made from Man shall trudge the courses of the earth, in fair weather and foul, and be tested at every tree and rough and bit that lies just six inches outside the railings. And they will forsake much for golf: money and time and family and all temporal ties, and though they may never become perfect, it is in their striving that they shall become good.

I can't prove any of this, of course, any more than any other divine: but it may just be that the Fields of Elysium are, in fact, a wondrous golf course, without hazard and where the eternal day is free alike of cloud and crosswind. And we shall all be reborn with short rubber legs and straight left arms and all those other things we lack on earth, and our swings shall be truly perfect and all our putts plumb-straight.

Of course, if you're anything less than scratch, you won't stand a chance of getting in. And even then, you'll have to know Somebody.

"*What happened? It bounced back on to the fairway and he got a par. That's what happened.*"

"Geoffrey! What on earth happened to your usual slice?"

"Do you really,—What's your handicap?"

GOLF WITHOUT GRASS

Henry Longhurst

GOLF, it has now long since been forgotten, is essentially a simple pastime wherein you start at A and hole out at B, overcoming as best you may such hazards as you encounter on the way, and I am always glad that this is in fact the way I started. My parents had decided to take their holiday in the little Dartmoor town of Yelverton and the year must have been 1921, since I so distinctly remember the man at Glastonbury, where we stopped on the way, with his monotonous chant of "*Old Moore's Almanack* predicts the coming events for 1922." The hotel at Yelverton overlooked the Common and here two other boys whose parents were staying there had carved out three holes with pen-knives. Soon I had acquired a sawn-off club and together we used to sneak out before breakfast and play two or three rounds. I became completely "bitten" by golf and, though I sometimes suspect that I ought to have put such talents as I possess to a better use, the game has been uncommonly good to me ever since.

Both playing it and writing about it began to take me to some of the best, and therefore best kept, courses in various parts of the world, and continuous visits to America ushered me into a world of vast country clubs with swimming pools, masseurs, barbers, and thousand-pound entrance fees. It is excusable, perhaps, if I came to forget about the original simple golf, the sort of golf that was good enough for that great writer, naturalist and fisherman, the first amateur champion, Horace Hutchinson, at Westward Ho! Where, if you found the hole becoming worn at the sides, you took out your pocket-knife and cut another, marking it with a gull's feather for the benefit of those coming behind.

I was brought back to the paths of truth and reality, and have not strayed since, by a visit to the oilfields in the foothills of Persia in the later stages of the war. New faces are always welcome in such parts—some fellows had not had leave for six years—and it was not long before I was ushered up to the Masjid-i-Suleiman golf club, named after the ancient temple nearby. The clubhouse was a fine granite affair, just like home, and the accents of Fife and Glasgow predominated amid the tinkle of ice on a Sunday morning. It was not the clubhouse, therefore, but the course which brought me, literally, down to earth.

Not a blade of grass was to be seen: only a miscellaneous assortment of stones, boulders and slippery mud which bakes rock hard in summer. The greens were of asphalt (the "pitch" mentioned in the construction of Noah's Ark) and covered by a layer of fine sand, each one of them being attended by a man with a long broom who smoothed out the surface before each player made his putt. As you could not stick a peg tee into the ground, the barefooted caddie boys, some of them quite enchanting little villains, turned up with a lump of clay, out of which they fashioned a tee like a halma man and presented it to you stuck on the bottom of the driver. Sometimes, as they departed for home, the lump of clay would conceal one of your golf balls. Some of the views were stupendous, and sights and sound not normally associated with the royal and ancient game enlivened the scene: a man in baggy trousers cantering across the course on a white horse, for instance, or half-a-dozen

Golf is being played very much in Egypt

women walking silently past the green with pots on their heads. *C'est magnifique,* I reflected, *mais ce n'est pas le golf.*

And yet it was. It took only a few holes to bring home to me that here, once more, was the original golf—from A to B, overcoming without complaint the hazards encountered on the way, the complete reverse of the modern conception of playing the same shot with every club in the bag, all 14 of them, and a good shot being assured of a standard result. Here, as in all desert golf, of which I now regard myself as something of an authority, you have to "manufacture" shots, as indeed you do on the Old course at St. Andrews. To cause a ball to carry an expanse of loose sand and pitch on a firm patch with just the right trajectory to run up through the gully and come to rest on a small circle of fast-running asphalt is true golf. Harry Vardon would have done it supremely well. Jack Nichlaus, I think, would not.

Later I went up to Teheran and here again the small European community had made a golf course. Not a blade of grass was to be seen and the course itself was absolutely plumb flat. The greens this time were of a thick variety of grit, or granite chippings, and very tiny, and a ball pitching on them left a dark, bare patch where it landed and stopped dead. Strings of grave, supercilious camels, roped together, would wander across behind the tee or between player and green, their bells clanging mournfully, the drivers huddled up asleep in rugs on the creatures' backs. As we finished our round, maybe a couple of hours later, they were still to be seen, specks on the distant plain, plodding on.

The emigrating Scots have carried golf to the farthest and most unlikely quarters of the globe. A doctor friend of mine, whose practice encompasses several thousand square miles of the Western Arctic, landed to visit some isolated Eskimos. Clambering over rocks and ice on some barren inhospitable island, he looked down and beheld, of all things, a golf ball. The answer, of course, was Scotsmen. The number of holes had coincided with the number of members: three holes, two Scottish engineers and a Jesuit priest.

Some years ago I visited Das Island, which juts almost imperceptibly out of the middle of the Persian Gulf, little more than a mile long and three-quarters wide—the base incidentally for an operation destined to raise a few hundred millions for the recently deposed Sheik of Abu Dhabi. Never mind the drilling barge, said the accents of Scotland. You must come and see our golf course. There, sure enough, after only three months were nine holes already laid out, the tees built, the greens marked out, and three Indian tailors hard at work embroidering nine flags with the

RESEARCHES IN ANCIENT SPORTS
The Lucullus Golf Club

Company's emblem. There was also, by a strange coincidence, Mr Terry-Thomas, the comedian, in whose company I later helped to eat a sheep in Bahrain.

Most of my grassless golf has been played, naturally enough, in the Middle East and many are the comical and poignant memories that return as I look back on it. The course of the Royal Baghdad Club is, or was, in the middle of the racecourse, and last time I was there the overnight rain had turned the alluvial deposit of which it, and indeed most of Iraq, is mainly formed into a kind of reddish glue. There were other excitements, however, since it was a race day. The jockeys ride half way out to the starting post and there dismount for a walk and a smoke while the public lay bets on the totalisator, which, shrewdly enough, they decline to do until they see that their selection is actually alive and on four legs. As we played the short seventh, we had an audience of half a dozen jockeys leaning against the rails, all indistinguishable from Charlie Smirke, as jockeys are all over the world. Their comments seemed to be of a derisory nature but we finished one up, we thought, when the first three of us got on the green and the fourth man hit the stick and nearly holed in one.

Hard by the Eternal Fires through which walked that imperishable trio, Shadrach, Meshach, and Abednego in the days of Nebuchadnezzar and your correspondent in more recent times—they are reduced to a few feet high now, but still stink as abominably of rotten eggs—you will find the Kirkuk Golf Club, the course broken up by a few eucalyptus trees and the terrain ideal for golf. A few years ago some bright spirit brought back from Cairo small quantities of a grass which it was hoped might not only survive the climate but also "creep". They made a miniature "green" on each "brown" and, when I was there, the eighteenth had already "crept" sixty yards back towards the tee. Perhaps the whole course is covered by now.

It was in Cairo that I had a mortifying experience of grassless golf in reverse. In the Egyptian open championship I was partnered at Gezira with a dignified sheik from a desert course, who played in a nightshirt, from below which a pair of enormous brown boots protruded like skis. He beat me easily. What really hurt, though, was his comment at the end. "That is the first time, sir, that I have ever played on grass."

Quite a wide experience of desert golf leaves me with a strong impression that the keenness of golfers varies in indirect ratio with the quality of the course they play on. In other words, the worse the course, the keener they become and the more seriously they take their game. I think of the arid waste of Aden, with the camels sweeping the greens in circles; of Kuwait, which is just one massive expanse of sand, but where you still cannot ground your club in a sand bunker; of Tripoli-super-Mare with the white city dazzling in the distance; and of Royal Benghazi, often inundated by the sea ("but it soaks through and improves the fairways") where a man told me of the house to which he proposed to retire beside a course in Hampshire and added solemnly "I have given my wife a power of attorney that, if the time comes when I can no longer play golf, she is to send for the vet and have me put down."

Above all, however, I remember El Fasher, in the heart of the Sudan, where they have nine greens, no tees, and one flag, which is brought out each time anyone wishes to play. No good having regular flags since, if they were made of wood, the ants would eat them and, if of metal, they would be instantly melted down by the locals for spears. A boy holds the flag in the first hole till one is near enough for an enormous Sudanese caddie to angle his bare feet behind the hole, whereupon the boy rushes off to hold the flag in the second. One short hole among some particularly repulsive camel thorn, sharp enough to use as gramophone needles, was described by the Governor as "set in a sylvan setting." As we neared the end, it was noticed that one of the caddies, wearing a blue diamond-shaped badge on the back of his nightshirt, was getting restive. It turned out that he was on ticket of leave from the local gaol and was anxious about getting back by lock-up. He was thereupon sent back in the Governor's car! I wonder if they miss the British after all.

ELSINORE GOLF CLUB

Golf must have flourished at Denmark in Hamlet's time, judging by the above reproduction of a very ancient Mural Decoration which has just come to light.

See Hamlet, Act II, Scene 2: ". . . drives; in rage, strikes wide."

GRAHAM'S GOLF CLUB

OH, GREAT PUTT!

THAT'S YOUR MATCH, THEN — 4 AND 3. WELL DONE, PETER!

I WAS LUCKY, DAD — I CAUGHT YOU ON ONE OF YOUR OFF-DAYS...
13

MIND IF WE COME THROUGH?
HONESTLY, SOME PEOPLE!

HOLDING UP THE WHOLE COURSE!
TYPICAL!

MEN ALWAYS SEEM TO TAKE IT SO SERIOUSLY!
12

I'M OFF THEN, DEAR!
COME ON, DICK— SHE CAN'T HEAR YOU!
24

NOT ABOVE THE NOISE OF THAT ROTOVATOR!

HOLD ON A MOMENT, TOM— I'LL JUST CHECK WITH ANGELA...

IT'S TOM PHELPS. ALL RIGHT IF I PLAY GOLF ON SUNDAY?
WHICH MEANS ME GETTING UP TO GIVE YOU AN EARLY BREAKFAST, I SUPPOSE... AND STUCK HERE ALL DAY WITH NO CAR... AND THE LAWN NEEDS CUTTING, AND IT WOULD BE NICE FOR THE CHILDREN TO SEE A LITTLE OF YOU FOR A CHANGE! HEAVEN KNOWS I SEE ENOUGH OF THEM WHILE YOU'RE AT THE OFFICE! AND HOW ABOUT THAT SHELF YOU WERE GOING TO PUT UP IN THE KITCHEN? BUT I SUPPOSE ANYTHING I SAY WON'T MAKE ANY DIFFERENCE.

THAT'S FINE, TOM— 9-30 ON THE FIRST TEE
7

"I suppose this means we'll have to cut across to the fifth."

BWANA GOLF

Chris Plumridge

When professional golfer Jimmy Stewart approached his ball for a second shot at the third hole he found a 10-foot cobra heading for it as well. He killed it—only to see another cobra, this time slightly shorter, emerging from the dead snake's jaws! It met the same fate. *Golf World*

IT was hot. He looked across the flat, baked African veldt and cursed the sun, the dust and flies. His hat, with "American Open Golf Championship" written across its front, was smeared with dirt and sweat.

"Christ!" he said, as he picked his teeth with a tee-peg, "why on earth didn't I stay on the nice easy American tournament circuit instead of coming out here?"

He leaned back in his mobile caddie-cart and reflected. He was 35 and at the zenith of his career. Leading money winner on the American tour, where he could drop a Sante Fe housewise in Bermuda shorts at 200 yards with a 3-iron or a Nassau businessman at 280 yards with a driver, he had the world at his spike-shod feet. Then Grabber, his manager, had told him he would never be considered really great unless he went to Africa. So he had come.

That was two years ago and here he was on his fiftieth safari, still searching for M'buru, the great elephant the natives called He-whose-tusks-are-thicker-than-Arnold-Palmer's-forearms. M'buru was an obsession, he must have him for himself to complete his Grand Slam. The Grand Slam consisted of a lion, a leopard, a rhino, a water buffalo and an elephant—he had bagged four of them but the elephant eluded him. Getting M'buru would give him the Grandest Slam of all.

That night they had pitched camp on the edge of a small donga (gully). Earlier, he had called for his chief caddie.

"Kidoko, come here you lazy nugu (ape) and bring my matched set of Scottish-made irons with the whippy shafts. I spy dinner out there."

Kidoko came running towards him, the big leather golf bag across his shoulders.

"Bwana", he said, a huge grin spreading across his dusky face, "is the Bwana going to shoot us some dinner?"

He looked at Kidoko with affection, the affection born out of two years of much laughter, a few tears and too many golf shots.

"Yes, Kidoko, I am going to shoot us some dinner."

About 100 yards away were a flock of guinea-fowl, quietly pecking at the arid earth. He selected a 4-iron, just right for a low trajectory and with enough power to do the job. He dropped half-a-dozen re-painted Dunlops on the dusty ground and took a couple of practice swings. The guinea-fowl were still unaware of his presence when the first ball took the head off the leading bird. The others stood stock still for about 20 seconds, during that time three more shots found their mark. The remainder of the flock shot off at high speed and he ceased firing. The native caddies rushed out to the dead birds and cut their throats with swift strokes of their pangas (knives).

"Not bad, eh?" he said to Kidoko, "Four out of four."

"The Bwana is truly a wonderful player", replied Kidoko, "we will eat well tonight."

And Kidoko loped off to help prepare the fires. He felt good, those four shots had reminded him of the four kilted Scotsmen he had downed on the sixteenth at St. Andrews when he had won his third British Open. He ate and slept well that night as the stars of the African sky twinkled like dew on the first green at Wentworth.

The messenger came at first light. He staggered into the camp, breathless and sweating.

"Bwana", he croaked, "I have seen him, not the length of Carnoustie from here, it is He-whose-tusks-are-thicker-than-Arnold-Palmer's-forearms as sure as God made little Gary Players."

A buzz of chatter rose from the natives and all eyes turned to the Bwana.

"Kidoko", he said quietly, "fetch my deep-faced driver with the stiff shaft." Kidoko came forward bearing the beautifully balanced hand-made club, the best St. Andrews could produce, and handed it to him. He felt the tacky leather grip in his hands and looked down the tempered steel shaft to the fine persimmon head—a feeling of almost sensual pleasure swept over him.

"This time", he thought, "this time I shall get you, M'buru." Then he walked over to the mobile caddie cart that Kidoko had already loaded with 3 dozen high compression Dunlop 65s and a gross of extra-long tee-pegs.

"We are ready, Bwana", said Kidoko.

"Right", he replied, "let's go!"

"Can't get out of this stuff with an eight apparently—give me the wedge."

They drove for about half-an-hour in the direction the messenger had pointed out. They drove in silence over the rough terrain and when they were 500 yards from a clump of mopani trees, they saw him. It was M'buru. The great pachyderm was resting in the shade of the trees, his tusks stretching out in front of him, a cloud of flies forming a black halo above his wrinkled head. Kidoko stopped the cart and they alighted, keeping downwind from the clump of trees that shaded M'buru. Kidoko silently handed him the deep-faced driver and a fresh dozen balls and they crept towards M'buru. They stopped 200 yards from their quarry and he set up the dozen balls on the tee-pegs.

He stepped back and checked his line, set himself up and with a preliminary waggle, swung the club in that lovely rhythmic motion that was known from Sunningdale to San Francisco and hit it. He hit it with a hint of draw to bring it homing in on M'buru's head at the soft point below the ear, but as soon as the ball had left the club he knew the shot was wrong. It struck M'buru just above the leg in the hardened muscle of the shoulder and with a trumpeted scream of pains, five tons of enraged elephant lumbered to its feet, trunk extended, questing for this threat to its existence. The great ears flapped and M'buru faced his tormentors. Another block-busting drive caught M'buru in the chest.

"Too low", he muttered. M'buru pinned his ears back, folded his trunk under to expose the menace of his tusks and charged. One, two, three successive shots thudded into M'buru's skull and he stopped, shook his head as if to clear his brain, then he crashed to the ground, rolled over and lay still. Kidoko exhaled through flared nostrils.

"Bwana", he said, "today you have slain M'buru, the one we call He-whose-tusks-are-thicker-than-Arnold-Palmer's-forearms. You are indeed a mighty golfer and I salute you."

"I see you, Kidoko", he replied, "and I salute you also. Let us go and examine the spoils of triumph."

When they reached the grey hulk that was one M'buru, the vultures were gathered in the surrounding trees, their hooked beaks sunk into the white collars of their necks.

"They look like greedy cousins waiting round a rich relative's death-bed", he said, "only this relative is dead and everything has been left to them".

He pegged a ball up and sent a shot clattering through the vulture-infested branches. They rose in clouds and circled wildly, squawking as they flew.

"Bloody aasvolës (vultures)", he said.

They had returned to the camp and sent the natives back to collect M'buru's tusks and cut up the carcass for fresh meat. It was a happy camp that night with much singing and drinking among them. Tomorrow he would have to begin the long trek back to the city and inform Grabber of his completion of the Grand Slam. He was not looking forward to it. Two years was a long time to spend in one country and during that time he had grown to love Africa and its myriad faces. No doubt that greedy little swine Grabber would have another circuit lined up for him, probably something in the Amazon basin, hunting anacondas. He sifted the remains of his drink in his glass and threw them into the fire. It had been a long day.

Kidoko and the others watched him load up the caddie cart with his two sets of clubs. They watched him as he placed M'buru's tusks in the back and their hearts were heavy.

"We see you, Bwana," they chanted, "we see you are going and our hearts are heavy."

"I see you too", he replied, "and my heart is also heavy, but I must return to the city and catch the great silver bird that drops from the sky and seek the land of my forefathers. You must go to your kraals (huts) and service your wives and tend your cattle."

They watched him, Kidoko and the others, as he drove off and their chanting grew louder.

"Aieee!" they wailed, "Bwana Golf, we salute you."

"Bwana Golf", murmured Kidoko, "he was a man."

Soon, all they could see was a cloud of dust on the horizon and the rattle of his clubs was no more.

"If only I'd bought that model hat, now would be the time to tell him about it."

Not What It Was

Golf as seen by Punch cartoonists at the beginning of the century

GOLF ON THE NORMAN COAST

THE GOLF STREAM

Flows along the Eastern Coast of Scotland during the Summer and Autumn.

THE ENGLISH WIFE

THE AMERICAN HUSBAND

THE DOCTRINE OF "HINTERLAND"

These three Gentlemen do not play the Game, but wish to take a Morning Walk by the Sea.

REAL ENJOYMENT

Non-Golfer (middle-aged, rather stout, who would like to play, and has been recommended it as healthy and amusing): "*Well, I cannot see where the excitement comes in in this game!*"
Caddie: "*Eh, mon, there's more swearing used over golf than any other game! D'ye no ca' that excitement?*"

"AMUSEMENTS"

Tennis Player (from London): "*Don't see the Fun o' this Game—knockin' a Ball into a Bush, and then 'untin' about for it!*"

A LAST RESORT

Miss Armstrong (who has foozled the ball six times with various clubs): "*And which am I to use now?*"
Weary Caddie: "*Gie it a knock wi' the Bag!*"

Bertie (to Caddie, searching for lost ball): "*What are you looking there for? Why, I must have driven it fifty yards further!*"
Diplomatic Caddie: "*But sometimes they hit a stone, Sir, and bounce back a terrible distance!*"

Licensed Caddie: "*Carry your Clubs, Sir?*"
Jones (who has chartered a small boy at a cheap rate): "*No, I've got a Caddie*".
Licensed Caddie: "*Carry your Caddie, Sir?*"

"KEEP YOUR HEAD STILL"
is the first rule in golf, and Binks means to do so.

GOLF NOTES

Old Hand: *"Ah, I heard you'd joined. Been round the links yet?"*
New Hand: *"Oh, yes. Went yesterday."*
Old Hand: *"What did you go round in?"*
New Hand: *"Oh, my ordinary clothes!"*

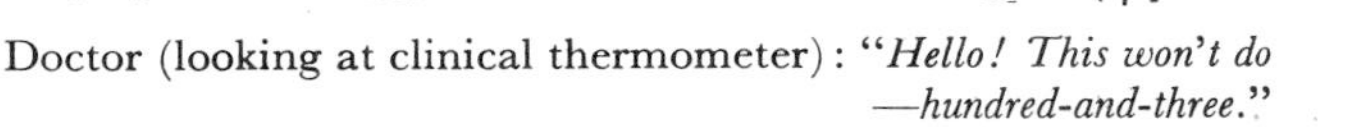

Doctor (looking at clinical thermometer): "*Hello! This won't do—hundred-and-three.*"

Golfing Patient: "*What's bogey?*"

THE MISERIES OF A *VERY* AMATEUR GOLFER

He is very shy, and unfortunately to drive off in front of the Lady Champion and a large Gallery. He makes a tremendous effort. The Ball travels at least Five Yards!

AN EXCUSABLE MISTAKE

Miggs and Griggs, who have got away for a week-end holiday, have strayed on to the Golf Links, and have been watching the Colonel, who has been bunkered for the last ten minutes.
Miggs: "*What's he doing?*"
Griggs: "*I dunno, Think he's trying to kill something.*"

A NEW DISEASE—THE GOLF TWIST

The 'Professor': "*Now a nice easy swing, Miss—and keep your eye on the ball.*"

A GOLFER'S NIGHTMARE

Cheerful Beginner (who has just smashed the Colonel's favourite driver): "*Oh, now I see why you have to carry so many clubs!*"

AND YET THEY EXPECT THE VOTE

Caddie: "*Say, Miss, we're just going to drive on to that green.*"

Aunty: "*Oh, thank the gentleman* so much *for sending you to tell us! Then we shall have a* beautiful *view!*"

1900

THE RULING PASSION

First Enthusiastic Golfer: "*I say, will you play another round with me on Thursday?*"

Second Enthusiastic Golfer: "*Well, I'm booked to be Married on that day—but it can be postponed!*"

1906

"*I say, do you know who's winning?*"
"*I think Uncle must be—I heard him offer to carry Aunty's Clubs.*"

Congestion on the Links

Congestion on the Links

THE RULING PASSION

Laden and perspiring stranger: "*Could you kindly tell me how far it is to the Station?*"

Sportsome Native: "*About a full drive, two brassies and a putt.*"

"My God, McGregor, what do you mean—it's only a game?"

A NATURAL ENQUIRY

"Mummy, what's that Man for?"

The teetotaller who did a Hole-in-One and offered "Cups of Tea all round".

A ROUND WITH THE PRO.

If any perfection
Exists on this earth
Immune from correction,
Unmeet for our mirth,

The despair of the scoffer,
The doom of the wit,
A professional golfer,
I fancy, is it.

No faults and no vices
Are found in this man,
He pulls not nor slices,
It don't seem he can;

Like an angel from heaven,
With grief, not with blame,
He points out the seven
Worst faults in your game.

"*You should hold your club* this *way.*"
He tells you, "*not* that."
You hold your club his way—
It hurts you, my hat!

Your hocks and your haunches,
Your hands and your hips
He assembles and launches
On unforeseen trips.

He says you should do it
Like so *and like* so;
Your legs become suet,
Your limbs are as dough.

He tells you to notice
The way his club wags;
(*But how* lovely *his coat is,*
How large *are his bags!*)

Golfer: "*What am I doing wrong now?*"
Instructor: "*Standing too near the ball—after you've hit it.*"

Tutor: "*The secret of putting is never to lift your head until you hear the ball rattle in the tin.*"
Pupil: "*That's silly. You can't keep gazing at the ground for the rest of your life.*"

You mark his beginning,
You watch how he ends,
You observe the ball spinning,
How high it ascends!

To you the whole riddle
Is just what he does
When he gets to the middle
And makes the brute buzz.

He tells you the divot
You took with your last
Was all due to the pivot—
Your comment is "Blast!"

He tells you your shoulders
Don't sink as they should;
Your intellect moulders,
Your brains are like wood.

But he *pulls his wrists through*
Right under his hands,
His whole body twists through;
Tremendous he stands.

He stands there and whops them
Without any fuss;
He scoops not nor tops them
Because he goes thus.

Obsequious batches
Of dutiful spheres
All day he despatches
Through Time and the years.

You copy his motions,
You take it like this,
You seize all his notions,
You strike—and you miss.

You aim with persistence,
With verve and with flair,
You gaze at the distance—
The orb is not there.

The hands have been lifted,
The head remains still,
Your eyes have not shifted—
No, nor has the pill.

He points out the errors
He told you before,
To add to your terrors
He points out two more.

Till, your eyes growing glassy,
Your face like a mule's,
You let out with your brassie
Regardless of rules.

And the ball goes careering
Far into the sky
And is seen disappearing
Due south, over Rye.

You stand staring wildly
(It's now at Madrid)
And the pro. remarks mildly,
"You see what you did?

You made every movement
I've tried to explain;
That shows great improvement,
Now do it again."

EVOE

"I say, d'you think I can go?"
"Go? Why not? There's no one in the bunker."

Across the Fairwa

"*You don't imagine I actually* enjoy *this aspect of my work?*"

"*A glance at your application form and I'll tell you whether or not we're on a waiting list.*"

"*And to think that fifty thousand dollars depend on a grown man getting that stupid little ball into that fatuous little hole in the ground.*"

nd into the rees

David Langdon

"Can't think how we'll manage to get an umpteen thousand quid order out of people who spend half an hour searching for a five-bob ball."

"Beautiful, sir. One of these days we'll let you try it with a ball."

"Blackballed. Complained to a member of the Greens Committee about the cauliflower."

"Anyone for golf?"

"Look at it this way—it saves you being trapped at home Sunday mornings."

"*I* still *say there must be something in the rules against it.*"

THE LINKS THAT SEVER

Think not I hold your love, my Susan, lightly;
Think not that my so firm affection fails,
Or that I deem your face has grown unsightly
That drew me swooning to the altar-rails;
Fear not that those pure ardours, O my sweet, wane
Which still recall the sun's meridian rays,
If round the links I recommend that we twain
Should go our several ways.

It is a game, this golf—ah, what a pity!—
Where true love's course is seldom smoothly run;
Where constant deviations from the pretty
Sunder the tracks that rightly should be one;
You on the sea-beach, I amid the heather,
Traversing totally divergent scenes—
Only by mere chance should we come together
Save on the tees and greens.

Rapture, I grant, would follow each reunion
That marked our eighteen separate journeys' ends;
After the horrid gaps in our communion
Meetings like these would make a fair amends;
But there's a risk that we might both be minded
To interchange salutes in lovers' wise,
And such a spectacle ere now has blinded
A modest caddie's eyes.

Or, on the other hand, there might be quarrels
If you should underestimate your score;
If, with a woman's sketchier sense of morals,
You made it twelve in lieu of twenty-four;
Your legend might arouse derisive laughter
Or in a peevish moment I might let
Fall some expression which for ever after
Both of us would regret.

Besides, the language of profound displeasure
In which I tell my clubs that they're to blame
Might shatter your ideal (and you, my treasure,
Possibly say the like when off your game);
Before each other, ever since our bridals,
We've said no word a saint might not repeat;
And we should loathe it if we caught our idols
Ending in putty feet.

What if the links without you will be lonely?
What if the parting cuts you like a knife?
We'll keep our mutual respect—the only
Sound basis of the perfect wedded life;
Though (as I mentioned) I shall sadly miss you,
I know the hazards, and I think it best
We should not stake our all upon the issue
Of quite so high a test.

O.S.

"Mr. Reynolds is no longer with us. He sank a long putt on the final hole to beat the manager."

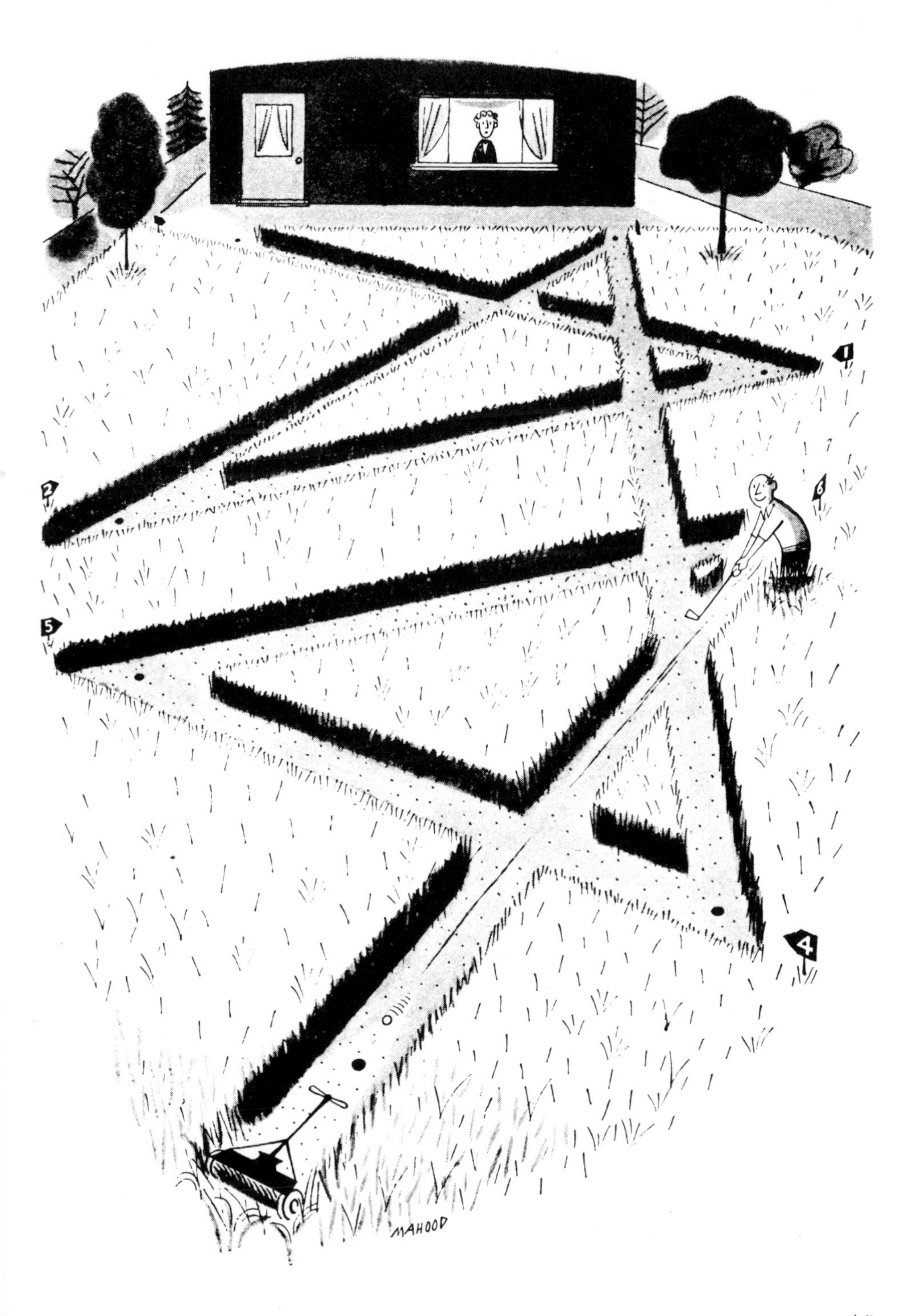
1
2
6
5
4
MAHOOD

The Golfather

Is the opening of betting shops at golf tournaments just the tip of the iceberg? CHRIS PLUMRIDGE breaks his vow of silence . . .

JOE 'Hot Wedge' Bananas was angry. He stormed off the 18th green after his last round in the Lasagne Classic, having just three-putted the last six greens to throw away the first prize of 250,000 dollars and free spaghetti for life. He slumped in the locker room, his mind a confused jumble. "It's no good," he said, "I just can't putt. Only the Golfather can save me now."

☆ ☆ ☆

Three hundred miles away in his heavily bunkered retreat the Golfather was holding court. Don Multio Paro was the Golfather. He had arrived in the country 40 years ago a nobody, a nothing pro hoping to scrape a living from the circuit. During those 40 years he had carved his reputation across the game to such an extent that his empire now extended from coast to coast. When a professional golfer anywhere holed a putt the Golfather knew about it and fast. Standing now in his living-room he looked an inconsequential figure until you noticed the steely blue of his grey-flecked eyes and the deference and homage those gathered around paid him.

The first supplicant shuffled forward. He was a small man wearing an old and rather shabby windcheater and water-proof trousers.

"Don Multio," he said, "it is I your brother's sister's cousin's husband who comes to see you about my daughter's hook."

"I remember you my brother's sister's cousin's husband and I know of your daughter's hook and how she came about it," replied the Golfather. "Those responsible have been taken care of, do not fear. But why, my brother's sister's cousin's husband, did you wait so long to come and see me? Why do you wait until you are in trouble before you visit your Golfather? Am I only to see you when things are not going right for you?"

The small man cringed.

"I am sorry, Don Multio, but I have been too busy with 20 lessons a day for the past two years, summer and winter. How else can a man like myself feed a wife and six bambinos?"

Don Multio looked at the small man with compassion; a thin smile crossed his lips.

"That doesn't tally with plate 4 of his chapter on putting."

"All right, my brother's sister's cousin's husband, go in peace, but one day I shall ask of you a favour and when I do you will remember this day."

"Yes, yes," replied the small man, "anything, Don Multio, you have only to ask and it shall be done."

With that the small man crept out gratefully from his audience with the Golfather, softly closing the door behind him. When the rustle of the small man's waterproof trousers had ceased in the passage outside, the Golfather turned to his lieutenants around him.

"No more audiences today, I am tired and my favourite Golfson is in trouble. That crazy boy 'Hot Wedge' has just three-putted the last six greens in the Lasagne Classic and he will be calling me shortly to arrange for me to get him in line. I need to concentrate, please leave me."

In another room of the Golfather's house, the telephone jangled.

☆ ☆ ☆

Joe "Hot Wedge" Bananas was nervous. He sat outside the Golfather's study anxiously waiting the summons to enter and twisting his golf cap in his hands as he waited. The door to the study opened and one of the Golfather's hatchet men beckoned him in. The Golfather greeted his favourite Golfson affectionately.

"My son," he said, "how wonderful to see you." The Golfather stepped back. "But you do not look as you used to, you are a little flabby around the waist, your eyes are bloodshot, your hands shake. Why? What has happened to you?"

"It's my putting, Golfather," replied Joe, "for months I haven't holed anything over six inches, my nerves are shot to pieces. The only hope I have is to get hold of a new putter being made down in the South, but the guy won't let me have one because of my connections with you."

The Golfather looked angrily at Joe.

"It is not just the putter that is stopping you, my son, it is more. You have been watched and your movements checked, you have been leading a fine old life out there on the circuit, women, drinking, playing cards, going to bed late. You have behaved like a guinea-wop and now you ask me to help you. You are not worth helping."

"Please help me, Golfather, just this time," whimpered Joe, "I promise you that

"Oh! What rotten bad luck, old boy!"

if you help me get this putter I will change my ways and get down to playing some serious golf on the tour, please help me and I promise you I'll be OK."

The Golfather motioned to one of his lieutenants. "Get this putter manufacturer on the phone and talk to him real nice about Joe here."

Joe clasped the Golfather by the hand. "You won't regret this, Golfather," said Joe, "but what are you going to say to the putter manufacturer?"

"Don't worry Joe," said the Golfather, "we'll make him an offer he can't refuse."

☆ ☆ ☆

The Chairman of the Southern Putter Manufacturing Company Inc. felt happy. He felt happy for two reasons. Firstly because he had put those guinea-wops in their place by refusing to supply them with a putter when they had phoned him earlier in the day. And secondly, because he had just locked up in his safe, the thing that he prized most—his solid gold, centre-shafted putter with the mink grip. As the Chairman of the Southern Putter Manufacturing Company Inc. got ready for bed he whistled a little tune because he was happy.

During the night the Chairman of the Southern Putter Manufacturing Company Inc. woke up with the feeling that there was someone else in the room with him, he reached out for the light and as he did so his hand brushed against something soft and furry. He switched on the light, his panic rising, and threw back the bedclothes. There, broken in a hundred pieces was his solid gold, centre-shafted putter with the mink grip. The Chairman of the Southern Putter Manufacturing Company Inc. opened his mouth in a long, agonising scream and his shrill ululations drowned the ringing of the telephone in the next room.

☆ ☆ ☆

Seated in the basement of his house, the Golfather was speaking on the phone.

"I told you not to worry, Joe," he said, "we just made him an offer he couldn't refuse. Now you go out there and start winning again. That's OK, Joe, be a good boy so your Golfather can be proud of you."

The Golfather put the phone down, turned to his indoor putting green and sank another putt.

"Sir! The general office is playing cricket!"

"What a day! Round in seventy-five and now this."

WATER THOSE GREENS IN SODOM!

The whole world will soon be fit for golfing holidays, reports eminent non-golfer E. S. TURNER

IT'S a pity about the Sodom and Gomorrah Golf Society's course at Kallia, on the Dead Sea. The clubhouse was burned down in 1948 and the course is no longer used. It was the lowest in the world—1,250 feet below sea level (I quote, as always, the *Guinness Book of Records*). Actually, it sounds like the biggest bunker in the world, but that's on a course in New Jersey.

Never mind, golfers will be teeing up again very soon in Sodom, if the vogue for golf holidays abroad persists. Meanwhile, there's nothing to stop teams of strong-winded golfers from setting off for the highest course in the world, 14,335 feet up at Morococha, Peru. There are courses where a man can find himself being barracked by kookaburras and squabbling for the ball with crocodiles. But don't expect to be welcomed, at every outlandish clubhouse, by a Scottish greenkeeper; they're more likely to be found in Spain and Portugal.

The fly-away golf holiday is a phenomenon of the last ten years. What's the attraction? For one thing, it can be cheaper to send a group of golfers to Iberia than to Scotland—and there's a guarantee of sun. Also, beyond the Pyrenees, the attractions include "crushed marble bunkers" (Sotogrande), "volcanic lava bunkers" (Tenerife) and other exciting novelties, not always geological; for example, cool drinks waiting at the 12th hole (Penina, Algarve).

No golfers roam more compulsively than the Americans. They're always filling in coupons which say things like: "I like the sound of your ad. Rush me full details about Gourmet Golf in Hawaii." A club professional can draw commission on any overseas booking he instigates. American groups of 200 and more are no novelty on the great dollar-spinning courses of Gleneagles Hotel, British Rail's Blenheim of the North. Last year Gleneagles welcomed the Chief executives Forum, an association of 150 dollar millionaires whose corporations were able to dispense with them for a week. President Eisenhower had a whimsical idea that nations could be brought closer by playing golf and his people-to-people groups, around fifty strong, fly over every year to play local teams at Gleneagles and Turnberry; in London they are based on the Savoy Hotel, always a good starting-point for promoting friendship.

The McCarthy Organisation of America sends over plane-load after plane-load of Americans to compete in Scottish tournaments (their wives tour the Trossachs and run amok in Princes Street). McCarthy's Seniors Tournament, for those of 55 and over, is limited to 192 competitors and has been a sell-out for years. This year the Arizona Golf Association, 110-strong, visited Gleneagles and Turnberry, and agreed to send 150 players per year for the next three years. (There's a course in Arizona with a rule: "If your ball lands within a club length of a rattlesnake you are allowed to move the ball," so it's not hard to guess the attraction of Gleneagles.)

It goes without saying that St. Andrews is an American colony too, but some of the pressure may be siphoned off when that Japanese entrepreneur, Zenya Hmada, has built his replica of the Old Course, complete with Swilcan Burn and Hell Bunker, in Japan. A great country for golfers, Japan, though the hobby is sometimes so expensive that a trip across the world to Gleneagles can seem a positive bargain.

Whatever the reason, Japanese golf groups are coming over more and more. So are parties from certain countries which were never designed for golf, notably Norway.

British millionaires are a stuffy lot. There's not much hope of getting 150 of them to go golfing round the world together. But Britain's middle-range managers could do worse than try the Dai Rees World Golf Tour this autumn. The advertisement says: "Visit the World Cup at Melbourne, with opportunities to play on major golf courses in Singapore, Sydney, Melbourne, Fiji, San Francisco and New York. Price £690."

Dai Rees comes in cheaper at Christmas. He is then resident at the five-star Hotel Dona Filipa in the Vale do Lobo, in the Algarve, and he will "talk and play golf with you" for a modest all-in figure. So will Dave Thomas and Jimmy Adams, also at grand hotels in the Algarve. Don't worry if you're a bad player—an English duke who invites tourists to dinner does not enquire about their table manners.

Dai Rees is on cordial terms with Global Tours, who are pioneers of the overseas golfing holiday. Now in their eighth season, they fly out 16,000 golfers a year. So far British groups are modestly sized compared with American ones. There's no shortage of aircraft or airports; the limiting factor just now is the number of beds available in golf hotels. Global think the traffic could be expanded to 50,000 movements—and that's a lot of people to play with Dai Rees. The leading European countries

"I should take your wedge, top it into the near bunker, and then offer 35s. 6d. per 10s. share ex the final dividend."

now welcoming golfers from Britain are Spain, Portugal, France and Switzerland. One likely form of expansion is in long winter weekend holidays, when British courses are unplayable.

A by-product of the boom is the founding of privilege-conferring bodies with names like Eurogolf and Golf International. The advantages are akin to those of joining the Automobile Association and the Diner's Club; your travel is eased, you live on credit and you collect discounts. (Don't ask why golfers should get cut rates from hotels and car hire firms—they just do.) If the hotel clerk sees a guest's Eurogolf tie, with its chaste golf ball motif, and his Eurogolf grip, similarly decorated, it will scarcely be necessary for him to flourish his card, entitling him to a cut rate, when settling the bill.

"*Tony Jacklin's divot.*"

Eurogolf's glossy 1972 Handbook is a feast of arcane knowledge. It describes some of the Great Holes of Europe. The 1st at Vimiero is "the most dramatic we have ever seen," with the tee 100 feet above the fairway and a fast-flowing river thirsting for every ball. Or there's the 7th at Vale do Lobo, "one of the most photographed holes in the world," requiring a 201-yards drive across three sea gorges. The compilers, among whom is Henry Longhurst, warn the player of holes which are "a bit out of sorts," just as guides to restaurants warn of cuisines which are going off.

If your friends think you are a philistine, picking up balls when you ought to be picking up culture, you could mention that you visited the old course at Dieppe, where English players used to complain of losing balls in a hairy depression which, with true English wit, they nicknamed the *bidet*. Claude Monet was so entranced by this spot that he painted it and gave it the title "Juno's *Bidet*."

Another good reminiscence for the 19th hole can be got at the Chiberta Golf Club, Biarritz, where you have "the opportunity of seeing the famous blind golfer Joseph Echeverria; he plays off an incredible five handicap and knows every blade of grass on the course." Follow this, after a suitable interval, with your tale about the course at Westward Ho, exclaiming with Eurogolf, "Where else are dogs trained to find lost balls by the smell of the paint?"

What about the language of golf? How do you shout "Fore" in Spanish? This isn't a problem, because the people in front of you, in Spain as in Scotland, are certain to be Americans. If you must show off, the French for green fee is *la cotisation*. But the rough is *le rough*, the bunker is *le bunker*, and so on.

There is a slight risk of being rebuffed at a foreign golf club, if you lack a special card or a letter of introduction. Golf club secretaries are turning out such letters all the time, certifying that the bearer is a man of honour and fit to be let loose in anybody's crushed marble bunkers. If you arrive on the same day as a group of Japanese tycoons, taking part in a Chief Executives' tournament, just go off somewhere and slice a few balls into the nearest natural *bidet*.

"I can tell you he's itching to get back to the office."

"Makes me sick! Runs a vintage car too".

Caddies and other Golfing Aids

As seen by THELWELL

"Try a number five iron".

A SHORT COURSE

GOOD THINGS ABOUT GOLF

Seeing Jack Nicklaus worry about a short putt.

Landing on the green thirty-six yards from the hole when your opponent is thirty-seven away.

Finding your opponent's ball in a rut in the rough and saying: "Bad news, I'm afraid . . ."

Hooking your drive on a hole which dog-legs to the left.

Hitting a seven iron shot all along the ground and stopping four feet from the hole.

Noticing that one of your opponents in a foursome is getting fed up with his partner saying "Sorry" all the time.

Bouncing off a tree on to the fairway.

Using a six iron at a short hole when everyone else is using a five.

Shouting "Fore!"

Getting on to a deserted first tee.

The two minutes after hitting a perfect shot.

Having no idea where your ball has gone and hearing your opponent say grudgingly: "Good shot".

Seeing your putt roll round the hole twice and stop. Then fall in.

Blasting out of a bunker and leaving the ball dead.

Hitting the pin, even if the ball does skid off into a bunker.

Chipping much too hard and seeing the ball mysteriously stop dead by the flag.

Driving further with your beaten-up stained old wood than your opponent does with his high polish Henry Cotton Fairwaymaster gadgetry.

Winning.

BAD THINGS ABOUT GOLF

Playing behind two ladies who are carefully not hitting the ball too far in case it goes out of sight.

Putting half an inch to the right of the hole and shooting off the green.

Finding your ball in the rough, only it has now got a slightly different trade mark and number.

Overbalancing when it's too late to stop the swing or pretend you've just pulled a muscle.

Hitting a perfect 3 iron shot, looking up and seeing the ball roll twenty yards and stop.

Bouncing two inches off the fairway into a mangrove swamp or gorse sanctuary.

Having to borrow tees off your opponent.

Losing a new ball while you've still got the crinkly shiny black wrapper in your pocket.

Hearing a cry of "Fore!" and not knowing if it's your last moment on earth or not.

Hitting the next shot after a perfect shot.

Driving a perfect drive over the direction post and finding your ball in a bunker which wasn't there last Sunday.

Chipping out of a bunker, well up into the air, landing on the top lip of the bunker and rolling back to where you're still standing.

Doing everything absolutely correctly and slicing out of bounds.

Finding that the only white dot on the fairway is a mushroom.

Developing a fault in your swing which is not mentioned in any of your nineteen books on golf.

Losing.

LEARN TO ENJOY GOLF IN TEN MINUTES

Playing golf well involves years of agony and is almost impossible. Enjoying golf can be achieved instantly. In this, the only manual ever produced, there is all you need to know.

GENERAL. It is commonly held that the purpose of golf is to play round eighteen holes in the smallest number of strokes possible. This misconception, which usually arises from watching the allied sport of professional golf, can lead to such disorders as persecution mania, obsession with parts of the body and golf lessons.

The true object of golf is to pass a pleasant Sunday morning at the club, and even out on the course. Once this has been grasped, everything else follows naturally—position of feet, swing, drinking and re-ordering. Above all, be relaxed.

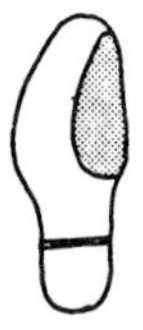

POSITION OF FEET. Note the left foot is on the left and the right foot on the right. Once this has been checked, you are ready to hit the ball, if you have not already done so.

N.B. Some golfers, when taking up position, concentrate on getting weight balanced equally between feet with slightly more on right heel, then on a half-turn of the hips, inward move of left knee, uplift of left heel, slow turn of wrists, firmness of right leg and downward pointing of right elbow. This usually causes them to fall over backwards.

SWING. It cannot be stressed too much that when addressing the ball, or pint, the golfer should furrow his brows in utmost concentration. Failure to do so will give an impression of arrogance or worse. During the backswing, slowly transfer the grim determination from the forehead to the chin and mouth, so that

The correct action: practice as often as possible.

at the moment of impact the player resembles Humphrey Bogart in a tight hole. During the follow-through, gradually relax the features. The final position should be one of almost mystical fulfilment.

SCORING. It often adds a certain interest to a round of golf to count your strokes as you go round, even to match them against your opponent's. If you find, however, that this leads to certain bad habits, such as swearing, over-drinking and practising, don't hesitate to give it up. It is always better to enjoy a disastrous round than to be heart-broken at going over par.

WIGGLE. A satisfying wiggle can provide some of the best moments in golf. Each golfer will develop his own methods of settling down for a stroke, but remember there are four basic areas for wiggling —feet, legs, shoulders and car-keys—and that they should not be activated together, or else the player will find himself hitting the ball before he is ready.

RUB OF THE GREEN. A certain amount of exaggeration about one's bad luck is permissible, but the direct untruth, or downhill lie, is not recommended.

CLUBS. A worthwhile golfer should never leave a club unlooked after. Nothing is worse than a barman who keeps beer badly or a pro who is never available.

FIVE VITAL RULES TO REMEMBER

18 (*b*) *A natural hazard, such as a wild slice or tendency to enter bunkers, shall be penalised by not less than six lost balls.*

32. *If a player finds the opponent's ball in the rough and secretly places it in his pocket, it shall immediately be returned to the rough.*

35 (*c*) *If a player shall have more than three air shots, he will explain that he is still having practice swings. This explanation will not be accepted.*

41. *Any player who buys a round out of turn shall not be penalised, unless he buys halves, when he shall be forced to take a round again.*

48. *When a player throws his golf bag in a pond and exclaims that he will never play golf again, he should immediately arrange with the resident professional to have the clubs salvaged for next Sunday's game.*

THE APPROACH

THE FOUR COMMONEST MISTAKES IN GOLF

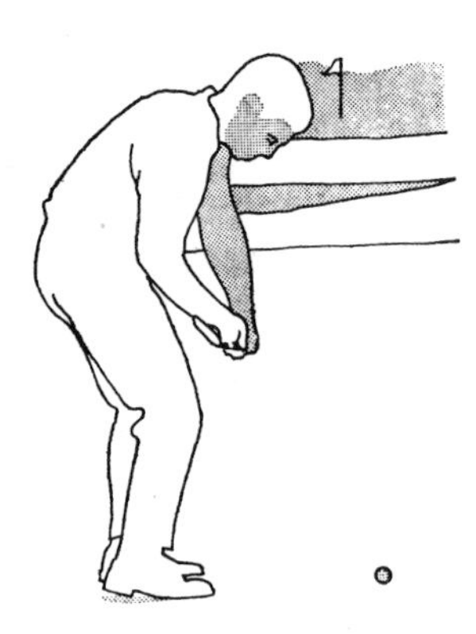

THERE is nothing wrong with this man's swing, except that he is not using a club. This fault can usually be traced to having thrown one's bag furiously into a pond and can easily be cured by giving up the game. (His white one-piece golf suit is unorthodox but permissible.)

THIS is the incorrect way of operating a beer pull. The arms are tense and the wrists stiff: result, a rushed action which produces too much froth and an unsettled pint. Remember to pull slowly, steadily and above all confidently, and keep your eye on the tankard at all times.

THE follow-through here is quite wrong. Instead of dashing off the eighteenth green towards the bar, the player should always clean his clubs, pay off his caddy, exchange condolences with his opponent and fix up a game for next week. Then *he should dash off the green towards the bar.*

THE player here has committed the elementary mistake of dropping his glass eye just as he is putting. This, of course, should be done as the other man is putting. The nuisance value is nil from the noise point of view; it must be done uphill from your opponent so that it rolls frighteningly into sight.

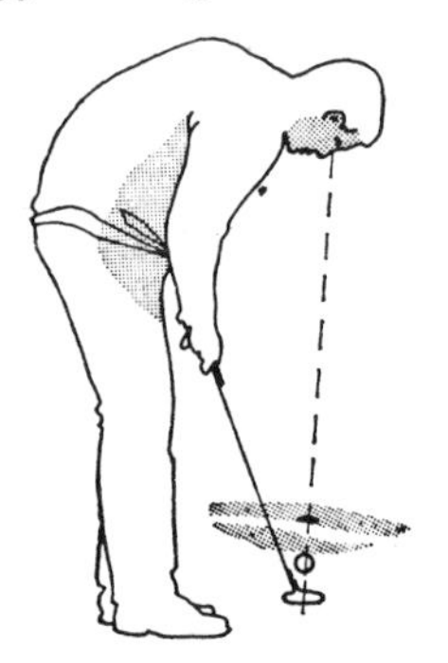

EARNINGS OF A TOP SUNDAY GOLFER

Like all modern games, golf involves financial risk and should be played by nobody who has forgotten to transfer his wallet to his golfing trousers. Here is a breakdown of the sort of earnings you should hope to attain to.

Gains	£	s.	d.	Losses	£	s.	d.
Average tournament prize money	0	2	6	Average tournament loss	0	2	6
Use of name for sponsorship of new members, exhibition bar tricks, etc.	0	7	6	Expenses for entertaining, travel, fruit machine	0	17	6
Investment in old golf balls found on course	0	5	6	Sixpence used to mark ball position	0	0	6
	£0	15	6		£1	0	6

Total loss 5*s*. In the top league losses of up to £5 can be sustained, depending on the price of whisky.

"She had to admit it was asking for trouble to start gardening in this."

Golfing Man

by LARRY

GARY PLAYER'S TEE
PICKED UP BIREDALE 1970
GOLF YEAR BOOK 1970

NEWS OF THE WORLD
CHILD GIVEN AWAY FOR SET OF GOLF CLUBS
Get Well Soon
SORRY YOU COULDN'T PLAY GOLF ON SUNDAY
PAR 4

"We came all the way down bumper-to-bumper."

UNDOING THE WHAT COMES NATURALLY *Chris Plumridge*

NOWADAYS, golfers are being continually bombarded with new theories and methods. We live in an age of programmed swings, the era of the natural player is past, lost in a welter of regimented uniformity. The question is, when will it all end? And the answer is, never. As long as golfers seek the Holy Grail of perfection they will continue to analyse, consult and alter their methods.

The golfer is constantly exposed to science—it lurks in books, articles, films and on the course. When Joe Exploder wins the Mesopotamia Open, the Bronx Classic and becomes leading money winner on the Falkland Islands' circuit there is immediately a book on the market called 'How I done it' by Joe Exploder. In the book, Joe explains that his game was up to maggots until he went to see an old Scottish professional named Rod McJigger. Dear old Rod told Joe that all he had to do was pronate his left wrist and adopt a right leg shin post. Joe followed these instructions and never looked back, hence the book, which, at £2.50 a throw, complete with action photographs, diagrams and a pull-out supplement of Rod McJigger's teaching fees, sells like binoculars at a strip show. Thousands of golfers devour Joe's words of wisdom and try to emulate him. What we don't realise is Joe has arms like a gorilla and can make sure the wind's behind him by just blowing his nose. In short, Joe's a pretty strong guy. So when we pronate our left wrists and adopt right leg shin posts the results are disastrous and painful—always providing we understand what on earth Joe is talking about in the first place. Whether we understand or not we are taken in, we reckon that if a method is good enough for someone like Joe then it must be good enough for us and it's only a question of applying science to our swings for us to start playing like Joe. As soon as we start thinking like this we are finished. Our minds become a confused mixture of different theories and the scientists have won again.

Where science really hurts is on the course. We can go out in the morning of a 36-hole competition and return to the clubhouse having recorded a fairly good score, but we are not happy. As we sit over our treacle tart and kummel we reflect on our round and work out where we could have saved shots. We deduce we weren't hitting our drives far enough, so all we have to do is make a slight adjustment to our swings and we'll knock six strokes off our score in the afternoon. The slight adjustment we make is based on what we think is sound knowledge of the game. When we start our afternoon round, however, we find things aren't going as well as expected and we

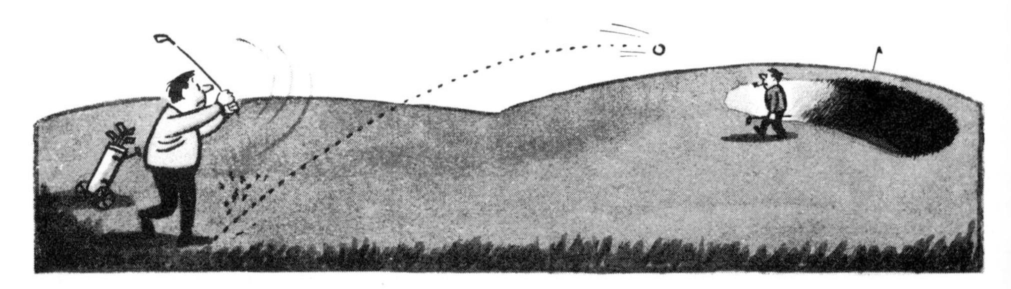

change another part of our swings. So it goes on until we can be seen somewhere in the vicinity of the 14th green making an early declaration to our innings. A classic case of too much science, even down to the treacle tart and kummel (we are led to believe these improve putting, though this has never been proved scientifically).

Further agony is inflicted when we visit the practice ground, where, while we are trying to eradicate a duck-hook of boomerang-like proportions, we are approached by the club theorist. He is usually a smallish man wearing owlish glasses who has made up for the lack of power in his game by embarking on an in-depth study of the swing, the clubs, how atmospheric pressure affects the flight of the ball and whether the wearing of braces helps for a bigger pivot. He is virtually impossible to beat off his handicap and never makes a mistake on the course. Anyhow, there we are on the practice ground, still flailing them quail-high in the direction of square-leg when the club theorist makes his presence known. The first inkling we have that the club theorist is upon us is the sight of a pair of white golf shoes (specially dulled to prevent reflection from the sun), with turned up toes (for greater leverage throughout the hitting area), and extra-long spikes (for gaining height to ensure a wider arc). We pretend we haven't noticed the white shoes and carry on determinedly. Then we hear "Tut, tut, such a pity to waste what could be a sound method". We look up and reply "What do you mean?" "Well", replies the club theorist "I would have thought it was obvious, your weight transference is all wrong, you're swinging too much inside, you're letting go at the top and you're not using your right hand at all." With that the club theorist moves off, leaving us to ponder on his words. When he is well out of sight we try and adopt his suggestions and, of course, as soon as we do this we are done for—doubt enters our minds and we end up with the most appalling slice or half-shank. Yet another victory in the cause of science and analysis.

What is needed to combat this obsession with science is a return to the natural way of doing things. Think what would happen if we analysed our eating methods—bent left arm, slow cutting action with the right hand, cock the left wrist before placing food in mouth—we'd probably end up by feeding our ears. And supposing we got the 'yips' with the fork, everything would shoot over the left shoulder with a frenzied jerk. This thirst for knowing why and how has got to stop. We've been conned too long, the scientists have had their way and now we must call an end to their gobbledegook. Look at it like this, did Einstein ever go round a rain-lashed Carnoustie in 71? Are the whole of the staff of NASA scratch-men? There's your answer. So let's go back to the natural way of playing golf and rely on natural flair to get results. Just to illustrate how futile all this theory business is, remember the man who tried the interlocking grip when he was cutting his wedding cake. He still only managed a slice.

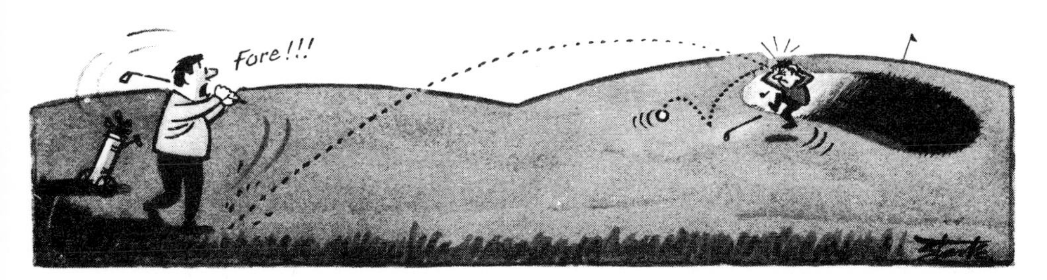

SOLID GOLD LINKS

DAVID LANGDON
Drives a hard bargain

"It's a toss-up between a vast housing development and a luxury golf-club."

"I'd like to trade in my new Tony Jacklins—he didn't do so well in the American Open."

"At 775,000 yen annual sub he just could not bear being upped to 24 handicap."

DAVID LANGDON

"This putt then for the £50,000 prize money and our side bet of a golf ball on the match."

"Aren't you going to block the sales of millions of centre-shafted syncro-steel putters with that old hickory favourite of yours?"

"Chap in Trap 30 just on his last bucket of 100."

"I thought you might be sympathetic to a second mortgage for my golf entrance fee and annual sub, sir."

Why are SOME bigger than OTHERS?

BEN WRIGHT on the ball.

GOLFERS have been concerned with the size of their balls for over fifty years. First they were too small for the Americans' liking, then the British realised the bigger one actually was better. Now the governing bodies on both sides of the Atlantic want a uniform, compromise or medium size ball. Where will it all end, a lot of golfers are asking themselves, if they are not past caring?

The trouble really started after the Autumn Business Meeting of the Royal and Ancient Golf Club of St. Andrews in 1920. By this time the members of the aforementioned club, henceforward to be known as the R & A, had long since appointed themselves as the government of golf, or more correctly the far from benevolent dictators of the game in Britain and throughout her dwindling Empire and Colonies.

The "feathery" golf ball, a mess of steamed feathers packed inside a heavy leather cover, had been superseded in 1848 by the only slightly more easily propelled "guttie", a lump of gutta percha moulded while warm, and painted white. In 1899 an American gentleman, name of Haskell, produced the first rubber cored golf ball, yards of fine rubber thread being tightly wound around a core or centre, and covered with a hard and durable plastic or vulcanised material.

The Haskell ball could really be made to fly, causing golf courses to be hurriedly lengthened accordingly. A really effective breakthrough was made in the scoring sense. Mr Haskell can hardly have appreciated the power of his influence on the entire golfing world. It was quickly obvious that something had to be done to standardise the ammunition, however.

At their Autumn Business Meeting of 1920 the R & A announced that: "On and after May 1st, 1921, the weight of the ball shall not be greater than 1·62 ounces avoirdupois, and the size not less than 1·62 inches in diameter". The United States Golf Association, hereinafter to be known as the USGA, were told rather curtly to make their own arrangements. And, being another body swollen by numbers of men with an obsession for power, and possessed of considerable delusions of grandeur, the USGA intimated to the eagerly waiting world in May 1929 that they had resolved to adopt "an easier and pleasanter ball for the average golfer". In plain words to hell with the British and their small balls.

Typically, some thought evilly, the Americans plumped for a ball they considered bigger and better than the British variety, henceforward to be referred to as the large and the small ball respectively. The Americans went for a ball of 1·68 inches in diameter and not more than 1·55 ounces in weight. In January 1932 the USGA changed the weight specification to 1·62 ounces to come grudgingly into some kind of line with the bloody British. So the two balls of differing sizes actually weighed exactly the same.

If you're still with me, and have never played with either the large or the small ball, you're probably thinking or asking what the hell difference does six hundredths of an inch in diameter make? You'd be surprised. And therein lies the crux of the matter.

The large ball is much more easily affected by the wind in flight. Sidewinds quickly blow it away, and it is very difficult to propel any distance at all into the wind. It has to be struck far more cleanly and decisively—driven forward rather than flicked—to stay on line. Because it also sits up visibly far better in the coarse Bermuda and other grasses prevalent in America the large ball is obviously far more suitable for use there, where golf tournaments are actually postponed or cancelled in rough weather we would call mild. The small ball, which is illegal in America, readily disappears in even short rough grass there. The large ball is more easily manipulated on and around the greens, since it stays on the clubface a fraction longer, and holds its line better on the putting surfaces.

So what is the point of using the small ball at all? The fact is that there is not a golfing hacker in the world who wouldn't willingly give an eye tooth for the privilege of being able to hit a golf ball ten or twenty yards further—such mortals are not the least interested in hitting it straighter. The small ball does, on average fly that much further than the large in normal conditions, and if hit really badly tends to fly straighter. In bad conditions of wind it bores through and holds its line much better. In that certain knowledge the British golf ball manufacturers have found it a complete waste of time trying to persuade millions of club golfers that they could play the game better, and eventually improve their standards by using the large ball.

Come off it mate, which goes further? Give me a dozen of them, then. The sale of large balls in Britain and elsewhere—only in America and Canada are small balls illegal—and highly prized by cheats, account for a pathetic three per cent of a multi-million pound market.

After many years of development of each ball on both sides of the Atlantic they became the polyurethane coated, liquid centred, snowy white bullets of enormous sophistication and compression on sale throughout the world today. The American manufacturers typically fought each other tooth and nail to produce the ball that would fly the furthest, so the USGA were forced to impose velocity restrictions of 255 feet per second in order not to see existing golf courses through the length and breadth of the continent rendered puny and anachronistic. But the British imposed no such velocity restrictions, which is why so many of our courses, and their bunkers have been outdated and put out of play.

Everything in both gardens was lovely enough until it became a matter of shattered British national pride to try to discover why the Americans had through the years become so much better at golf than ourselves. For instance since the biennial Ryder Cup contests were instituted in 1927 between teams of professionals of both countries we have won but thrice, in 1929 and 1933 in Britain before the Americans caught on, and in 1957 at Lindrick. On the last occasion the Americans chose a distinctly weak team, perhaps to encourage us. In the Walker Cup matches between teams of amateurs from both countries our performances have been far worse until recently. Until we finally won back the Cup amidst scenes of startling hysteria and relief at St. Andrews last year the British had only once previously been successful—in 1938—since the firstly annual, and then biennial fixtures were instituted in 1922. In similarly styled Curtis Cup matches our women have only twice been successful since 1932. We have never won any of the three Cups on American soil. And since the Second World War only four home bred professionals, Fred Daly in 1947, Henry Cotton, 1948, Max Faulkner, 1951 and Tony Jacklin, 1969, have won the British Open Championship.

"Good Heavens! You really were killing a snake."

Of course anyone with even average intelligence might have deduced that, since their population is roughly three and half times the size of ours America or Americans have to start favourites every time they tee it up against us. But it was Arnold Palmer, who won our Open Championship in 1961 and 1962, Jack Nicklaus, 1966 and 1970 and Gary Player, 1959 and 1968 who really rocked the boat by saying repeatedly that British golfers could never be the equal of those playing regularly on the American tour with the large ball, until they adopted the 1·68 inch variety themselves. Tony Jacklin was to bear out these words by winning his first American tournament at Jacksonville, Florida in 1968, returning to win the British Open in 1969, and then taking the US Open the following year in "British" weather in rural Minnesota. The fact that Jacklin has both the guts and the skill to win tournaments even when playing with a piece of furnace coke was conveniently overlooked.

The British Professional Golfers' Association adopted the big ball compulsorily for a trial period in 1964 in selected tournaments, but dropped it at the end of the season because the climate did not seem suitable, and scores soared so high that the paying public stayed away. They didn't want to see "those mugs play—half of them can't break 80".

But the Americans went on winning, so in their infinite wisdom our PGA re-adopted the large ball for a three years trial period in 1968—and are still using it in all tournaments in Britain—but not in Europe, which is quite ridiculous, and has caused a rebellious faction to press for the abandonment of the "experiment" forthwith, and an immediate return to the small ball.

Results have improved dramatically since the large ball was adopted, however. In 1969 the Ryder Cup match at Royal Birkdale ended in a thrilling tie at 16–16. There were those—and I was one—present who opined we could have won had the right team been fielded on the final afternoon by British captain Eric Brown. In 1971 in St. Louis, Missouri we lost 16–11, with five matches halved, but might easily have won had not Brown, captain again, surrendered a hard-won initiative—we led 4–3 at the end of the first day's foursomes—by inexplicably resting two of our best players, Jacklin and Brian Huggett from the following morning's fourballs, when we were whitewashed 4–0.

In 1970 Tommy Horton became the first ever British professional to win the South African Open Championship—played with the small ball. But it is generally agreed that it is childs play to switch from the large to the small ball, the latter being so much easier and less demanding to play. It is the reverse process that poses the problems—at least initially.

Now the logical step might well have been to leave well alone, and allow the large ball eventually to become the official competitive ball for tournaments and championships the world over. But the R & A and USGA have never been strong on logic, and they felt it was high time to assert their authority again before things got out of hand. They decided unanimously that a uniform size ball was desirable on all counts, since golf is about the only world sport currently played with ammunition of differing sizes.

On the surface this is indeed a ludicrous situation. But the way the governing bodies went about correcting it was even more ridiculous, and has almost certainly caused the failure of the scheme. The Joint Committee formed to investigate the possibilities of a uniform ball didn't go for a 1·65 inch ball, exactly to split the difference. They went for a 1·66 inch ball with a velocity restriction of 250 feet per second. But what was so incredibly stupid and naïve, they tried to face the golf ball manufacturers virtually with a fait accompli. They chose to announce that after conclusive tests—these were laughably amateurish, and immediately exposed as such—the Joint Committee had proved the inarguable advantages of the 1·66 inch ball, and planned to introduce legislation to introduce it as the only legal ball in the world.

Golf ball manufacturers on both sides of the Atlantic were first amused, then amazed, and then downright angry at this presumptuous effrontery. In plain words the American manufacturers told the USGA they would refuse to manufacture such a ball until they had carried out conclusive feasibility tests themselves to prove its advantages. The British stood similarly firm alongside them as the full and awful implications of the move were realised. Re-tooling and re-moulding would cost manufacturers millions of dollars and pounds for two hundredths and four hundredths of an inch in America and Britain respectively. And who would pay for all that? Yes, of course it would have to be the dear old public, the poor unfortunate hackers of the world.

Well, the American manufacturers have carried out, and are still producing evidence to prove conclusively that the compromise 1·66 inch ball has none of the advantages claimed for it by the USGA and R & A. The latest meeting of the two governing bodies took place in Buenos Aires during the recent Eisenhower trophy competition, and I quote: "for further important discussions on the proposal that the Rules be amended in order to introduce a ball of an agreed minimum size, and other specifications, in all countries throughout the world from a date to be decided in due course.

"As a result of a constructive meeting, the USGA plans to have further discussions with interested parties before the end of the year."

For interested parties read golf ball manufacturers. And if I know the latter gentlemen, an extremely able and level-headed bunch, they will tell the USGA what to do with their compromise ball. If they don't do so, then it is high time that golfers everywhere united to tell the self-styled governments on both sides of the Atlantic to leave golfers and their balls alone, and let's get on with the game.

Women at Golf

"They must be ours—we're the only two people playing."

"No counting the score, understand!"

thelwell

"Before we married you conceded putts twice *this long."*

"That's better! I managed to keep on the fairway this time!"

"*Hurry up. Other people are waiting to use the bunker.*"

"*I was standing too close to the ball, my grip was all wrong, I wasn't keeping my head down, and what else . . .?*"

"Hold it! I don't think it's going to be a lost ball after all."